The Connemara I

The Connemara Pony: purcha

Comprehensive coverage of all aspects of buying a new Connemara pony, stable management, veterinary care, costs and transportation.

by

Julie Anderson

ALL RIGHTS RESERVED. This book contains material protected under International and Federal Copyright Laws and Treaties.

Any unauthorized reprint or use of this material is strictly prohibited. No part of this book may be reproduced or transmitted in any form or by any means, electronic, mechanical or otherwise, including photocopying or recording, or by any information storage and retrieval system without express written permission from the author.

Copyrighted © 2015

Published by IMB Publishing

Table of Contents

Table of Contents 3

Introduction 4

Chapter 1: The Connemara Pony 6

Chapter 2: What to buy and where to find your Connemara pony 10

Chapter 3: Trying horses for purchase 18

Chapter 4: How to keep your Connemara pony 22

Chapter 5: Vetting before purchase and insurance 24

Chapter 6: Bringing your new Connemara pony home 36

Chapter 7: Care of your Connemara pony 39

Chapter 8: Grassland and Stabling 55

Chapter 9: Exercise and ridden work 62

Chapter 10: Routines – daily, weekly, monthly 72

Chapter 11: Minor Ailments 75

Chapter 12: Saying Goodbye 98

Chapter 13: Costs 107

Chapter 14: Travelling horses 123

Conclusion 131

Glossary 132

Introduction

Introduction

Horses have been an integral part of the life of man for well over one thousand years, first as a food source and then as a work mate whether ridden or driven. Now horses are mainly involved in our lives for pleasure and for sport, they are companion animals; some ridden, some not. In the United Kingdom, there are thought to be as many horses now for leisure purposes as there were before the outbreak of the Great War a century ago.

Horse and ponies are generally defined by their breed or type and their height and are measured in units called hands; each hand is equivalent to four inches. The measurement is taken from the ground to the withers; these are the bony, spinal processes located at the bottom of the neck just in front of where the saddle would sit and at the bottom of the mane, which is the long hair on the neck distinct from the coat.

A horse is classified as any animal that measures 14.3 hands high so 14 hands and 3 inches or above (149cm). Anything beneath that height is classified as a pony so 14.2 hh (hands high) or smaller (148cm). There are some very small breeds of pony, the Shetland pony from Scotland in the United Kingdom and the Falabella which originates from Argentina although it is important to note that the Falabella is not classified as a pony but rather a miniature horse despite its height, which is often no more than 8 hh (81 cm). Miniature horses are a distinct grouping of animals generally no taller than 34-38 inches (86-96cm). These animals are technically of pony size but are grouped as miniature horses as in every way they are perfect replicas of much larger animals. The Shetland pony however is defined as a pony and is the smallest native breed of pony in the United Kingdom. The Shetland Pony Society also now has a sub category for miniatures as do some of the other native breeds in the UK.

Introduction

This book is designed to lead you through the process of acquiring your Connemara pony although much of the content about care and management will be applicable to all breeds of horse and pony. It will cover the route you need to take to acquiring your perfect animal and explain the costs and time commitment required to care for your new pony, plus outlining some of the hazards and pitfalls along the way. There is a useful glossary at the back which provides details of breed societies and appropriate organisations referenced in the text plus definitions of some of the most commonly used abbreviations. It is not intended to be an exhaustive guide but an overview, giving you enough detail to seek further information elsewhere on specific topics.

Chapter 1: The Connemara Pony

Chapter 1: The Connemara Pony

The Connemara pony takes its name from a most beautiful and remote part of Ireland located on the West coast. Connemara is described as the real emerald of Ireland. The Connemara pony is the sole "indigenous" equine of Ireland.

The origins of the Connemara pony are not clear. Some believe that the when the Spanish Armada sank off Ireland's western shores in 1588, the horses on the galleons which would have been Andalusians, swam to shore and bred with the native stock running wild in the mountains. Others claim that the origins of the pony date back much earlier to Viking times.

The forerunner of the Connemara was a hardy, agile pony called the Irish Hobby which was prevalent in Ireland in the sixteenth and seventeenth centuries. The Hobby had influence from both Barb and Spanish breeding. Arabs were imported in the nineteenth century and various government breeding schemes also brought in Welsh Cobs, Thoroughbreds, Hackneys and the less than desirable heavy horse, the Clydesdale, in an attempt to arrest degeneration in the native Irish stock. There were also Irish Draught sires and a line to the famous pure-bred Arab, Naseel.

Chapter 1: The Connemara Pony

The Connemara Pony Breeders' Society "CPBS" was formed in 1923 with the backing of Ireland's Department of Agriculture with the intention of improving the breed. The English Connemara Society was founded in 1947. The first stallion to be entered in the Connemara Stud Book was Cannon Ball, foaled in 1904. He won the Farmers' Race at Oughterard for sixteen years in succession. A pony called Rebel, foaled in 1922 and Golden Gleam, foaled a decade later, also had powerful influences on the breed development.

Connemara is wild, remote and harsh, it is a place of bogs and lakes and also mountains and rugged terrain. This natural environment has given the pony hardiness, endurance and its special character. The Connemara pony was used for every sort of farm task as well as being employed as a pack animal to carry seaweed, potatoes, peat and corn. Of the old type of pony, Professor Cossor Ewart wrote in the Royal Commission report in 1897, "they are capable of living where all but wild ponies would starve…strong and hardy as mules, fertile and free from hereditary disease, their extinction would be a national loss".

From these origins, comes the modern Connemara pony. Here are some of the breed qualities and features that you should look for in a good Connemara pony:-

- The head of the Connemara pony is small and neat revealing the influence of oriental blood in the pony's ancestry. The forehead is broad with ears of pony size
- The length of rein is exceptional in the Connemara, this essentially means the length of the neck although this should not be so long that is out of proportion to the rest of the body
- The pony should show a good, sloping shoulder and an open and well-proportioned front which make it ideal for riding
- The body should be compact and noted for its depth, the body should be deep with a strong back

Chapter 1: The Connemara Pony

- The pony's action is that of a true riding pony which is why it has become so popular as a performance animal; the pony should move freely from the shoulder without undue knee action, the stride should be ground covering
- Feet, like the other native breeds, are hard and strong and the Connemara pony is very sure footed
- The Connemara can stand between 13 hh (132cm) and 14.2hh (148cm)

Usual coat colours are dun, grey, black, bay, brown and occasionally, roan. Piebalds (black and white) and skewbalds (brown and white) are not accepted by the Connemara Pony Breeders' Society.

The Connemara is a brilliant performance pony. The Connemara is fast, courageous, sensible and a remarkable jumper. Because of its size, the Connemara pony is very popular with older children and small adults and can make a wonderful and versatile mother/daughter share. The Connemara is also a popular cross with the Thoroughbred as this produces an excellent sports horse with all of the toughness and resilience of the Connemara pony and the added speed and athleticism of the blood horse. There are also Connemara pony influences to be found in some of the Irish Draught breed lines. The Irish Draught horse is a larger, heavier breed which originates from Ireland and was originally used for farm work and then, with the influence of Thoroughbred breeding, became outcrossed to produce lighter, faster horses which are now used as sports horses. It is possible to see traces of Connemara within these modern sports horses as Connemara pony breeding was often mixed in with the Irish Draught bloodlines.

Connemara ponies have been exported extensively to Europe where they are very popular and are now bred in considerable numbers. In Germany, the pony is subject to rigorous performance testing, a tenet that underpins much of the German attitude towards breeding good quality stock of any type.

Chapter 1: The Connemara Pony

In the United Kingdom, prestigious county shows run a range of classes for the Connemara pony both ridden and in hand and there is also a nationwide series with the other native breeds leading to a final at the Horse of the Year Show in October and one of the most coveted competitions, the Mountain and Moorland Championship which is held at the London International Horse Show every Christmas. This is one of the most hotly contested events in the UK amongst native pony breeders and owners and ponies qualify all over the country throughout the year for this event.

As already stated, Connemara ponies make excellent jumping ponies whether in pure show jumping competitions or as working hunter ponies. There are specific classes for native working hunter ponies in which the Connemara pony will compete against other, similar sized native breeds such as the New Forest pony and the larger Welsh Sections C and D. A 22 year old Connemara gelding named the Nugget famously cleared a fence measuring 7'2" (2.18 metres) at the International Horse Show at Olympia in London in 1935. And in 1968, a Connemara cross Thoroughbred called Stroller won a silver medal in the show jumping section of the Olympic Games in Mexico. This pony and he was a pony as he measured in at 14.1hh (145cm) won 61 International competitions in his lifetime.

Connemara ponies do not have the same popularity as driving ponies as some of the other native breeds. This is not because they are not suitable to break to harness but rather that they make such good performance ponies that they tend to be found most strongly in the ridden disciplines. The largest display of Connemara ponies in the world takes place at the Clifden Show in County Galway on the third Thursday of every August. The show has been organised by the Connemara Breed Society since 1924 and hundreds of ponies attend, it really is a unique event. Breeders, owners and producers from all over the world gather together to indulge themselves in all things Connemara, competition classes and also buying and selling all mixed together with that unique Irish hospitality and enthusiasm for the horse.

Chapter 2: What to buy and where to find your Connemara pony

Although this book is about Connemara ponies, I think it is important to first look in general terms at how to make a decision about what type of horse or pony to buy before looking in more detail at acquiring a Connemara. There are various criteria to consider when buying a horse. Firstly, there is currently no legal requirement in the UK to have a licence if you own a horse. There is however a requirement in Eire to have a licence for each horse you own. There is no listed requirement in the USA but this may vary from State to State so it is worth checking this on a more local basis. If you are importing a horse then there will be import requirements and legalities that you will need to follow, particularly with regard to disease status. In much the same way that you choose a car or a house, the animal needs to fulfil a particular role and satisfy certain criteria and so it is worth listing out a specification on a piece of paper. Here are some useful headings to consider:-

- Height
- Age
- Colour
- Type or breed
- Gender
- The rider's/owner's ability

Height

It is not unusual for people to over horse themselves or their children by buying an animal that is simply too big, this is particularly so with children where further growth is anticipated. Nothing will destroy the rider's confidence more quickly than riding a horse which is too large and becomes too much for the rider. It is worth remembering that it is not just the work under saddle but also all of the handling issues which can become problematical if the animal is simply too big for the rider. Each animal has to be considered on its own merits and conformation and the horse's way of going, schooling and age are relevant when considering a particular horse or pony – height should not therefore be taken in isolation.

Age

It is my absolute belief that young horses those six years or less, are for professionals or at the very least, highly experienced riders. The education of a "green" or novice horse requires an awful lot of knowledge and expertise and not least of all, time. The average horse owner does not need to buy a youngster and therefore should confine their search to animals which are over the age of six. Older more experienced horses and ponies often make an ideal purchase for the first time horse owner, indeed many small ponies circulate through different families for years as they are outgrown by their riders and passed on. If they are extremely good at their job for example a child's first pony, they are worth their weight in gold; you will not often see them advertised for sale as word of mouth usually secures their next home.

Colour

Colour is really a matter of personal preference. Some people have strong likes and dislikes but a horse should never be chosen or rejected solely on its colour. Remember the saying, "a good horse is never a bad colour". Some colours can enhance the appearance of a horse so always look twice at a grey horse – other colours such as skewbald and piebald can appear to suggest conformational issues that are misleading just because of the way in which the horse is marked. Some colours in certain types or breed of horses and ponies may attract a premium price because they are considered desirable, other colours or markings are considered distinctly undesirable and will have the opposite effect.

Chapter 2: What to buy and where to find your Connemara

Type or breed

The type of horse to buy depends very much on what job it is going to be asked to do. The only type of horse worth putting on a racecourse is a full Thoroughbred; you wouldn't get very far with anything else. There are other types and breeds of horse which are favoured by certain disciplines, the Thoroughbred or part-bred for eventing and the continental warmblood for show jumping and dressage. A horse that is going to be something of a jack of all trades, maybe hacking, some hunting, riding club and pony club would be described as a riding club horse, a family horse or as an all-rounder. This type of horse can manifest itself in the guise of many different breeds or cross breeds and does not necessarily come in one particular shape or form.

The way a horse or pony is put together is described as "conformation" and an animal's conformation will to some extent dictate its suitability for a particular job. For example, a small pony of cob type will have a short, powerful neck and may therefore prove too strong for a small child rider. However, like height, the issue of conformation can never be taken in isolation; the pony may be well schooled and of a very genuine temperament and therefore prove not to be a strong ride at all despite its appearance. Conformation will also influence the likelihood of the horse or pony staying "sound" i.e. free from lameness. Therefore, conformation is an area your instructor will be particularly interested in when you are assessing an animal for purchase and it may also be commented upon by the vet during the pre-purchase examination.

Gender

Much like young horses, stallions should only be contemplated as a prospective purchase by the professional yard or owner. Whether to buy a mare or a gelding is again a matter of personal preference.

There is an idea that a mare is always a better purchase than a gelding because if anything goes wrong then it would be possible to have a foal from her. Breeding should never be undertaken

Chapter 2: What to buy and where to find your Connemara

lightly not least because there are far too many unsuitable and poorly conformed animals which are the products of ill-thought out breeding projects contributing to a looming welfare crisis, certainly in the UK. Foals should only be produced from mares of quality which have proved themselves in their chosen field and are sound in their conformation and temperament; a mare should not be bred from simply because she has broken down with an injury or issue that makes her no longer suitable as a riding horse.

The ability of the rider

The rider should have a minimum level of competence in their riding before contemplating buying a horse, i.e. secure and balanced in walk, trot and canter and if relevant, jumping small fences. You should have ridden outside and feel competent hacking out a quiet horse. Remember, riding school horses are kept in a very routine existence and know their job well; they are generally also selected for their temperament and docile nature. Privately owned horses, horses kept outside the riding school environment, are not the same as this and it is important to try and expose yourself to a wide variety of animals before you embark upon buying your own if you have only had experience of riding school horses. You may have friends with suitable horses that you can ride or get involved with and there are always a plethora of advertisements in saddleries and on social media for people to help out with care and exercise. But beware of putting yourself in a dangerous position with an unsuitable animal and you should always have appropriate personal accident insurance.

In addition to the riding ability described above, you will also need to have competence and confidence to care for a horse correctly in areas such as feeding, grooming, handling the horse for the farrier, worming, first aid, handling, travelling and saddler. Your local riding school or livery yard may offer appropriate stable management courses which can help you gain the necessary skills and knowledge. Local equine and agricultural colleges also offer short or evening courses for amateur riders and owners who wish to increase their knowledge of stable management. A good instructor should be able to offer you a lot

Chapter 2: What to buy and where to find your Connemara

of advice and support in the management of your horse but they cannot be there every day so the responsibility for that horse care will ultimately rest with you as the owner.

It is not uncommon for people to overestimate their riding ability when they are trying horses for purchase so you do need to make an honest assessment of your strengths and weaknesses. Take with you an instructor who knows your riding well and who can also ride the horse for you prior to purchase. They should then be able to advise you as to whether they feel the horse is a suitable choice for you in terms of type, way of going and temperament.

If you buy the wrong horse then you will have to manage and upkeep that animal until you are able to sell the horse on or find an alternative home. If you can't actually manage the horse and/or are unable to ride it then you will encounter enormous problems when trying to sell and you will then be stuck with an animal that you don't want. Sadly this situation is not uncommon and will usually result in financial loss to the owner at the very least either by selling on at a lower price or incurring the cost of obtaining professional help to try and sort out the problems. Worse, a happy outcome for the horse is usually the last thing on people's minds when they find themselves in that situation. Many horses are passed from pillar to post, sold on for ever-decreasing amounts of money to another unprepared and ill-informed person.

If you do buy the wrong horse then admit it and get professional help immediately. Your first port of call would normally be an experienced instructor who should then be able to advise you of the options in your particular situation. If you have made a mistake in your purchase, that is not the fault of the horse and you have a duty to make sure that the horse is then re-homed into a more suitable and appropriate environment. This may well involve you in additional expenditure that you will not recover. The importance of taking appropriate professional advice at the time of purchase to avoid this scenario cannot be emphasized enough; you might lose money but the horse has no-one to protect it and many of these animals eventually end up in welfare

Chapter 2: What to buy and where to find your Connemara

charities through no fault of their own – and these are the lucky ones.

Finding a Connemara pony

Pure bred Connemara ponies can be obtained from many different sources. You may know of a local breeder or a post to a Facebook page or Internet search will easily identify where the studs are in your area or further afield. Alternatively, you can contact the Connemara Pony Breeders' Society, "CPBS" who should be able to provide a list of breeders and their locations. Breeders are usually happy to accept visitors or you can view their stock on line or at shows and events.

In the normal course of events, most people looking to buy a horse would look locally in the first instance either on line at websites like Horsequest or Horsemart or at adverts in papers, journals and their local tack shops and feed merchants. If you are looking for something specific however, in terms of breed then you may find that you will have to travel further afield and that there is nothing available to buy in your local area.

Whether to buy or loan your Connemara pony?

Not everyone buys their horse or pony, some people are quite happy to loan. Caring for a Connemara pony whether you own it or not differs little in practical and financial terms but it is worth examining the decision-making process that leads a person to conclude that a purchase is more appropriate to their situation than having a horse or pony on loan. Here are some examples where it has been decided that either a short or long term loan will be more suitable than a purchase.

- A much treasured and elderly Connemara pony has started to succumb to old age and has some wear and tear issues in the forelimbs; she is often unlevel and sometimes lame. The pony will be mostly retired and only used for very light hacking from time to time when sound. The younger replacement, a two year old, bought in anticipation of this day, is growing nicely in the field. However the youngster

Chapter 2: What to buy and where to find your Connemara

is a good eighteen months away from being backed and so in the interim period, the owner is looking for a suitable horse on loan which can be returned when the youngster has been broken in and is riding away.
- An eventer with a tendon injury is expected to make a full recovery but a replacement is sought on loan by the rider so that a promising career can continue without interruption.
- A young boy is toying with the idea of riding but is not quite as keen as his sisters; a family friend offers the perfect outgrown lead rein pony for a few months to see whether the child really wants to ride sufficiently to justify a purchase at a later date.

Whether to loan or purchase a Connemara pony is really a matter of personal preference - loaning a pony avoids the initial expense of purchase but as anyone who keeps horses knows, the main costs lie with keeping the animal over several years not with the purchase.

Loan and share agreements are very common in the equestrian field but they need to be approached with caution as they lack the clarity of the sale situation and often fail due to misunderstandings and poor communication.

If you are going to contemplate a loan then it is important to have a well-executed loan agreement that sets out clearly the rights and responsibilities of both parties, there are templates available online or from organisations such as the British Horse Society which you can customise to suit your needs and circumstances. These cover all sorts of eventualities such as accidents, vets fees, terms of return of the animal and also possible purchase after a set period of time. There are many potential areas for disagreement and dispute within a loan situation and it is the job of the loan agreement to reduce these if not remove them altogether.

If you are looking for a Connemara pony then it may prove quite hard to find a loan arrangement, although not impossible. Some Connemara studs will loan out non-breeding stock, animals that

Chapter 2: What to buy and where to find your Connemara

they wish to keep ownership of but do not wish to show or breed from and it is an arrangement that can work well for both parties. Sometimes studs like to place their Connemara ponies with competitive homes as this seeks to further advance the name and reputation of that establishment and so they may be less interested in an arrangement that is just going to keep the animal as a pet essentially. However this can be attractive as a route to re-home older Connemara stock, for example brood mares that have finished their breeding careers.

And finally, the law in the United Kingdom makes a distinction between buying from a private seller and buying from commercial businesses sometimes known as dealers. It is very much buyer beware when buying privately and it is completely up to the purchaser to find out everything he can about the horse. In a commercial sale, the buyer has greater protection at law in the UK under the Sale of Goods Act that the animal is of merchantable quality and fit for the purpose intended.

Chapter 3: Trying horses for purchase

Once you have found a Connemara pony which appears to fit the criteria you have set for your purchase, then you will need to make an initial enquiry, probably best done by phone call. Depending on where you have seen the pony advertised you may also have seen a photograph and in some cases, video footage.

The purpose of the initial enquiry is to find out as much as possible about this Connemara pony in order to determine whether or not he merits viewing in the flesh. You might therefore find it helpful to list out some questions and then to record your findings as you go along as, there could be too much detail there for you to recall, particularly if you have more than one pony to phone up about. Below is listed some of the information that you will be looking for.

- Height
- Gender
- Colour
- Age
- Temperament
- Type or breed, any breed society registration
- Papers and/or passport
- Way of going or ride
- Past experience both schooling and competitive
- Recent work in the last 6 months, current fitness
- Previous/current rider, their level and experience
- Any vices? Bucking, kicking, rearing, napping, weaving, box walking, cribbing
- Handling, turning out, catching, loading, shoeing, clipping, veterinary treatment
- Hacking, alone or in company, travelling, traffic
- Any health issues

Chapter 3: Trying horses for purchase

- Are vaccinations up to date
- Keep, living in or out or part and part
- Current feed
- Reason for sale
- How long has the pony been in its current home
- Price, negotiable or not, does the price include any tack or rugs
- Where is the pony located, trial facilities

Once a Connemara pony has been found that appears to be suitable following this initial conversation then the next stage is to go and try him.

Before trying the pony, you should ensure that the vendor can provide you with suitable facilities where you can ride in safety. The pony could possibly be a youngster and not therefore broken to ride but you should still always see the pony move in walk and trot even without a rider. The riding facility does not have to be an arena although that would be the most ideal, a small fenced field is sufficient providing that it is not muddy. It is not a good idea to try unknown horses in large open spaces. If you want to try the horse over fences, make sure that there will be some jump wings and poles available for you to use.

If you are intend to purchase this pony as a riding pony then you should tell the vendor that you would like to see them ride the pony first and then your instructor will ride followed by you or your appointed jockey. Ask them not to tack the pony up until you arrive so that you can see for yourself the pony's behaviour and the way in which they handle him. Once the pony has been ridden, you should ask the vendor whether or not you can trot him up for soundness and you will need a suitable area of hard level ground to do this, a quiet road will do if necessary. Some people trot the horse up even before they ride it on the basis that if it appears unlevel or not sound then the viewing will cease at that point.

Chapter 3: Trying horses for purchase

You should expect to spend a couple of hours on a first visit to ride and consider the horse and then many people will ask to come back again in order to hack out or alternatively, you may wish to do this once you have ridden the horse in an enclosed area. However, never hack an unknown horse out alone; ask the vendor whether they can arrange for someone to ride with you. Whatever you want to do on that first visit, you should make plain to the vendor so that they are clear as to who is coming and what you will want to do with their horse, this is a matter of courtesy as well as practicality.

When you try a new horse, you need to find out as much information about him as possible as you may well have to make a decision when you have dismounted, subject to vetting of course. If the horse is nice and well-priced and there are other people interested in purchasing then you may not even have the luxury of sleeping on a decision.

It can be quite daunting trying new horses in front of an audience and working the horse without any guidance or instruction from the floor unless you are experienced in schooling horses on your own. Take your instructor with you and he/she will be able to guide you through different school movements and transitions so that you are best able to utilize the time available to make an accurate assessment of the horse. Discuss the horse afterwards with your instructor and listen to their advice.

In some cases, the vendor may agree for you to have the horse "on trial" for a specified period. Trial periods are perhaps less common than they used to be and are fraught with difficulties for both parties. If a vendor is happy to let their horse go out on a short trial then they will usually state this in the advertisement.

If a trial period is offered by the vendor and is something you would like to take advantage of then the arrangement should be regulated in writing. Both parties must be clear how long the trial is for, where the horse is to be kept and what activities are to be undertaken during that time. It is particularly important from an

Chapter 3: Trying horses for purchase

insurance perspective that liability for any injury or accident is laid out in black and white.

You should make sure that any decision to purchase and subsequent agreement is made subject to the horse satisfactorily passing a pre-purchase vetting. This will help prevent you from buying a horse that is ill or unsound at the time of purchase but it does not act as a guarantee for the future health of the horse.

Chapter 4: How to keep your Connemara pony

Before you contemplate buying your Connemara pony, you will need to make a decision as to where you intend to keep him. It is worth noting that horses are herd animals and are sociable creatures, they like the company of other horses and will suffer if they are kept in isolation. Horses can also mix well with other animals – donkeys, cattle, goats, sheep, fowl – but whether they will or not is very much down to the personality of the individual animal and generally, they will always prefer the company of their own species.

A good livery yard will provide you with the level of care and facilities that you might need for your Connemara pony, with experienced staff on hand to help you but a decent livery yard will not be an inexpensive arrangement and the more they do for your horse in terms of care, the higher the monthly bill will be.

You may wish to livery your Connemara pony on what is called a part-livery basis whereby you are responsible for some of the daily care routine but not all or, you may wish to opt for what is called DIY livery or "Do it Yourself" livery whereby the yard owner provides the basic facilities and you as the owner of the horse are responsible for all of the care.

The decision as to which type of livery you opt for is usually based on time available and financial resources but a first time owner would be wise to consider full or assisted livery in a good yard in the first instance, an arrangement which can alter as time passes and more experience and knowledge is gained.

Some people view it as the ultimate to keep their horse or pony at home and this obviously reduces some of the cost element quite considerably but it can be a very isolating arrangement. You will

Chapter 4: How to keep your Connemara pony

need sufficient experience or someone who can advise you on a regular basis and not just with the care of the horse but also in sorting out fencing and pasture and if necessary, stable design and construction. It is very hard to replicate at home the type of facilities and back-up which are available on a good commercial yard. However, there is nothing quite like looking out of the window at your own Connemara pony grazing in the meadow!

You should have sourced a good yard or have your facilities ready at home before you start searching for your new Connemara pony. A good professional livery yard will be happy to show you around on more than one occasion and you should be asked to read and complete a contract setting out the service that will be provided to you and which party is responsible for what. Be cautious of a yard that does not set out its terms in writing.

Chapter 5: Vetting before purchase and insurance

Before buying your Connemara pony, it is advisable to get a vet to check the pony over for any issues or ailments and there is a formal process to do this called a Pre-Purchase Veterinary examination. The procedure that this process follows in the United Kingdom is laid down by the Royal College of Veterinary Surgeons "RCVS" who govern the veterinary profession in the UK and "BEVA", the British Equine Veterinary Association. Speak to a local veterinary practice or other owners to discover what the process is in your country or state.

There is no such thing as a perfect horse but you should know what you are buying and a vet can conduct an examination of your Connemara pony and discuss with you whether the pony is fit for the purpose intended. Also, if you intend to insure your Connemara pony then some insurance companies will insist on a vetting prior to insuring for certain classes such as loss of use. Always speak to your intended insurer before undertaking a vetting so that you know exactly what they require from you.

Vetting doesn't just apply to purchasing a horse, this can also be relevant in a loan situation; remember the bulk of your costs will come when looking after the animal and under a loan agreement, you are normally liable for vets fees so a veterinary examination might help you to make a decision about whether or not to take a particular Connemara pony on loan.

It is the responsibility of the purchaser to request and organize a pre-purchase vetting although many vendors when they are advertising will use the phrase "open to vet". If they don't state this, you are still entitled to request a veterinary examination, remember the old adage of "caveat emptor" or "buyer beware" - it

Chapter 5: Vetting before purchase and insurance

is up to you as the purchaser to find out as much as you can about the horse before buying it.

If you are buying a Connemara pony locally then your own vet or one recommended to you can conduct the examination, if you are buying further afield then as the purchaser of the animal, you will be expected to instruct a veterinary surgeon yourself. Usually if you are out of your area, your own vet through their network can recommend a practice close enough to the location of your intended purchase or even an individual contact who can go out and conduct the examination.

Sometimes purchasers will offer their own vet who has cared for the horse as a candidate to conduct the examination. There are mixed views on this. Some would say that a vet who knows the horse well is the best person to discuss issues with you and the professional code of conduct prevents vets from behaving in an inappropriate or deceptive manner. However, others would point to an inherent conflict of interest. It is most common practice that the buyer will source and instruct their own vet.

It is ideal if at all possible that you are present when the vetting takes place as the vet can discuss things with you there and then and point out specific issues such as perhaps a soundness problem, which may be harder for you to evaluate over the phone later on. Even if you cannot be present on the day, the vet will want a conversation with you prior to the vetting and clear instruction from you as to the intended use of the Connemara pony; clearly there are issues or problems which might be relevant to a high performance horse that would not trouble a pony being purchased as a pet.

Some Connemara ponies will be offered for sale with a vetting certificate in place, this can happen if a previous buyer has withdrawn from purchase and the vendor will use it to help promote another sale. Insurance companies will usually accept a vetting certificate that is less than six months old but again you will need to check this specific point with each insurer that you contact for a quote. Even if the insurance company is happy to

Chapter 5: Vetting before purchase and insurance

accept the certificate, you still need to consider whether you would like your own vet or a vet under your instruction to vet and discuss the horse with you whilst you are present.

The main vetting procedure for pre-purchase examination is described as a five stage vetting and it takes about an hour and a half to complete. There are five clear components of the examination. These are as follows:-

1. Clinical observation of the horse at rest. This is usually carried out in the stable and the vet will palpate or feel all four of the horse's limbs and listen to the resting heart rate and the lungs. The vet will also examine the horse's eyes with an ophthalmoscope in as dark an environment as possible, usually by just closing the top door of the stable. The horse is then taken outside and stood square and an assessment is made of conformation as this can indicate or predispose to issues with gait and soundness once the horse starts moving. The condition of the horse is also noted as this indicates work levels and fitness.

2. Lameness assessment. This involves walking and trotting the horse in hand on a hard, level surface in a straight line and then also observing the horse trotting on both reins, to the left and right, again on a hard surface on a small circle, usually of 10 metres in diameter. There is an option at this point to flexion test the horse which involves flexing the front and hind limbs in turn for about a minute and then immediately trotting the horse away in a straight line to see if this reveals any lameness issues. Flexion tests can be controversial and some vets dislike them on the basis that any animal over a certain age will show some reaction to them purely on an age related basis whereas other vets take the view that finding out as much as you can about the horse is best practice. The lameness assessment is done early on in the examination so that if the horse is not sound i.e. lame then the examination can cease at that point and most vets will only charge a proportion of the fee if that occurs. Routine shoeing or trimming can make some horses sore so it is usually better not to present a horse for a pre-purchase vetting within 7 days of a visit from the farrier.

Chapter 5: Vetting before purchase and insurance

3. Strenuous exercise. Next, the vet will want to observe the horse after strenuous exercise involving trotting and cantering. This work is usually undertaken ridden. If the horse cannot be ridden either because there is no rider or because the horse is not yet backed which means it is not yet broken in to ride, then the horse may be lunged instead. Lungeing is a process whereby the horse is exercised around a person standing on the ground by means of a long line called a lunge line. Lungeing forms part of the early education of the horse and is used as part of normal ridden work in the programme of an established horse. If neither lungeing nor ridden work is an option, the horse may be loose schooled which is essentially exercising himself in a schooling area. The vet will check the horse's heart rate and respiration again after exercise and particularly monitor how quickly it returns to the resting rate following exercise and pertaining to that horse's level of fitness. He will also listen to the horse's wind, which means the horse's airways to hear whether the horse makes any noise when doing faster work.

4. The horse is returned to the stable and observed at rest to see if anything comes to light as the result of the exercise. It is usually at this time that the vet will check the horse's passport and also record the horse's markings on a chart which will form part of the report to the purchaser.

5. A second trot up is then performed to establish that the horse has remained sound after exercise. Some vets simply undertake this in a straight line and do not repeat the work on a small circle and the flexion tests; others repeat all of the second stage again. Finally, a blood sample is taken; this will not be tested but will be stored for 6 months and then destroyed if not needed. This blood sample will be checked for the presence of pain relieving drugs such as phenylbutazone should there be a dispute between the purchaser and vendor after the sale of the horse. Phenylbutazone or "bute" as it is commonly referred to is a non-steroidal anti-inflammatory drug which also offers pain relief and this could be used to mask a range of conditions thereby deceiving the potential purchaser that a lame horse is in fact sound and fit for purchase.

Chapter 5: Vetting before purchase and insurance

For high value sports horses, other diagnostic tests can be offered to the purchaser prior to sale and these include X rays usually of the hooves, ultrasonography and endoscopy. The latter is where an examination of the horse's airways is made via a tube called an endoscope which is passed down the windpipe or trachea. Clearly for very high value horses and horses performing at national and international level, these tests may be of benefit as they can give more information about the horse performing in a highly demanding athletic arena. The average horse owner should however find all the information they need via the five stage examination.

There is at the other end of the spectrum, a shorter examination called the Two Stage vetting which takes anywhere between half and three quarters of an hour. This is in essence, the first two stages of the full five stage vetting only. Some vets may ask you to sign a document stating that you understand the difference between a two and a five stage vetting and are happy to proceed with the shortened version. A two stage vetting will include a blood sample.

The cost of a full five stage vetting is anywhere from £150 to £300 ($235-$470). If you are asking a vet to travel outside their usual area of practice to vet your prospective purchase then it is normal to pay additional travelling costs as well.

There is no such thing as a perfect horse and your vetting is bound to reveal some issues or cause for comment, the key thing is deciding whether or not these things are relevant to what you intend to do with your Connemara pony. That is why it is so helpful being present on the day so that the vet can show you things as they arise and discuss them with you face to face.

A pony may therefore pass the vetting for your purposes if you intend to keep the Connemara pony just as a pet but the report form may contain several observations which could fail the pony in other circumstances e.g. if it was required as a performance animal. If a horse fails the vetting clearly at any point during the examination – for example, it is hopping lame - then you are still

Chapter 5: Vetting before purchase and insurance

liable for the vet's fee incurred up to the point at which the examination ceased.

If you are a novice or first time owner, you should take someone knowledgeable with you when you go to the view your Connemara pony; they can ride the pony first and cast their eye over it for any obvious issues. If you have an instructor then they are the perfect choice as they know you and your riding skills and abilities and what type of horse is likely to suit you. A good instructor can have the horse trotted up in front of them and if anything arises from that then this would clearly be a horse that you would not want to put through the time and expense of a five stage vetting.

Vices

Horses are described as having vices if they exhibit one or more of the following:-

- Bucking
- Rearing
- Bolting
- Napping
- Biting
- Cribbing and wind sucking
- Weaving
- Kicking
- Pacing or box walking

A horse bucks when it puts its head in between its front legs and lifts both hind legs off the ground. This is common behaviour when the horse is at liberty in the field but is less desirable under saddle. A horse may also kick out whilst he is bucking and this is called fly bucking. Rearing however is the opposite and this is where the horse takes his front legs off the ground sometimes to a high level and balances totally on his hind legs. Some horses will actually go right over backwards when rearing hence the reason why this is considered to be one of the worst

Chapter 5: Vetting before purchase and insurance

vices. A horse that rears regularly and has an established habit is called a "confirmed rearer".

Bolting is when a saddled horse gallops off with a rider and refuses to come back under control. And napping is when a horse refuses to leave another horse or a particular area or place such as the yard when going out for a ride or the collecting ring at a show for example.

Cribbing is where the horse grabs a solid object with his teeth; the stable door is a favourite choice and chews or "cribs" on it. Some horses do this and simultaneously inhale air, these are called wind suckers. Horses can also do this in the field on wooden fencing or even on wooden fence posts. Horses that crib often leave telltale signs such as chew marks on their stable door although it is possible to fit a metal strip to deter them. They also have teeth which are badly worn down. Horses can be aged with varying degrees of accuracy by their teeth which erupt continuously throughout their lives but a horse that cribs would give quite a confusing assessment to someone who didn't know the history of that animal. And finally, weaving is when a horse moves the front part of his body from side to side – this may be seen at feed time although some horses will do this more frequently.

Vices are clearly undesirable but some are more undesirable than others. The odd buck going into canter or a horse that weaves just at feed time is not going to cause an undue amount of concern but a confirmed rearer or a bolter is quite another story. It is also important to differentiate between vices that take place whilst the horse is under saddle and which have the potential to put a rider into danger and those which take place in the stable. A horse that bites or kicks when you put its rugs on is not necessarily pleasant to deal with but it is a manageable issue in the right hands. Many competition riders forgive their horses all sorts of unpleasant and unwelcome behaviour in their private lives because of their prodigious talent within the competition environment.

Chapter 5: Vetting before purchase and insurance

The vetting process does not include any reference to vices and so it is sensible to make these enquiries with the vendor. Many vets will advise you to include a written warranty which in the UK will offer you some protection under the Trade Descriptions Act if you are buying privately. A warranty can be a simple question and answer tick box list, does this horse buck? Does this horse rear and so on. Once the vendor has been asked the question, he may not misrepresent the facts and if you do need to rely on a misrepresentation at a later date, then it is much easier to evidence this by way of a written document rather than a verbal conversation which then boils down to one person's word against another.

A written warranty can also include other information such as:-

- Will your Connemara pony go in both a horse box and a trailer or only a box? Will he travel in a trailer with the partition in or does he prefer to travel without the partition and stand diagonally? This means that you could never travel this pony with another and this could be quite relevant to your future plans
- How does he behave in traffic?
- What is he like to clip? Does he require sedation as that will mean calling the vet out each time he is clipped
- What is he like to shoe?
- Will he hack out on his own or does he have to be in company?

Day to day handling or behaviour of the horse can make or break a lifelong partnership so these are all very important questions to ask.

Insurance

There are four types of insurance to potentially consider when buying your Connemara pony and these are:-

- Full cover of the value of the pony including vets fees

Chapter 5: Vetting before purchase and insurance

- Cover for vets fees only
- Third party liability
- Personal accident cover for the rider/handler

Many people choose to insure their horse upon purchase. Insurers will insist on a five stage vetting if you have a high value animal or you want loss of use cover for example. There are many different aspects of full cover and many different providers in the market place. A quick Internet search or scan through the pages of the Horse and Hound magazine will reveal many companies and there is a comparison website run by the Horse and Hound where you can compare insurance quotes from different providers.

Equine cover is a bit like any other form of insurance; you can choose essentially the different component elements of the policy depending on your requirements. You can choose to insure the value of your Connemara pony so that you receive the declared value of the pony on the policy if the worst comes to the worst, subject of course to the policy's terms and conditions. To this you can add loss of use cover which is applicable where you have a performance horse for example, who is unable to continue a competitive career due to illness or injury but does not need to be put down. Again subject to terms and conditions, your insurer should pay you the value of the animal.

You can also insure your Connemara pony for claims against vets fees; like all insurance policies this will be subject to a policy excess per individual claim and financial limits on the maximum which can be paid out per claim. Once a claim has been commenced for an illness or injury, the usual terms are that the insurer will cover costs arising from treatment for one year only for your horse and then that particular issue will form the subject of an exclusion on the policy. For example, a condition or illness relating to one limb of the horse will usually result in an exclusion going forward that no further claims can be made for that particular problem or similar or related problems in the future for that limb. Exclusions may be lifted at a later date providing the

Chapter 5: Vetting before purchase and insurance

horse has not experienced a repeat episode and subject to negotiation with the insurance company underwriters.

To an equine policy, you can add cover for your Connemara pony's tack and for your horsebox or trailer if you have one. As with any insurance policy, it is imperative that you read the terms and conditions very carefully; too many people get caught out when they are expecting cover and it isn't there and if this occurs at a stressful time when your horse is ill or injured then this can make a difficult situation even worse. And perhaps the other mantra to remember is, if it seems too good to be true then it probably is! Cheap cover is not always what it seems and you really do get what you pay for.

As with all insurance cover, you can pay an annual premium or monthly installments by Direct Debit. An equine policy is negotiated annually and premium rates will change not just depending on your claim history, as that is dealt with by way of exclusion, but by the age of the horse and what you are doing with it which may vary from year to year. And of course, the value, which can alter depending perhaps on competition successes or breeding record.

At the point of renewal each year, you will be asked to complete a health declaration for your Connemara pony giving details of any issues that may have occurred during the past year. The insurer asks for this information as you may not have made any claims but your horse might still have been treated by a vet and this is information that the underwriter will need to know. If you make a claim then the insurer will request your horse's veterinary records in any event so any issue that has not been declared previously will come to light at that point and you run the risk of invalidating your cover for withholding information.

If you have a Connemara pony on loan then you may only want cover in place for vet's fees. Any mortality value will not be paid to you but the owner of the horse with the exception of a rescue horse which some insurers will deem to have no monetary value. The insurance company will need sight of your loan agreement or

Chapter 5: Vetting before purchase and insurance

at least a letter from the person loaning the horse to confirm the arrangement. The cover offered is the same as that on an ordinary full policy for vet's fees.

You may also be offered third party liability cover which is to protect you financially in the event of a claim because your Connemara pony has got loose or strayed and caused an accident for which you are liable. Some organisations such as the British Horse Society (BHS) offer this as part of their most expensive membership package but you need to read carefully the parameters of the cover, as it may be limited to injury or damage to property caused by your horse in a recreational situation only. So for example, an incident that occurs in a competition situation by your horse may not be covered.

Personal accident cover is the final element of insurance protection that you may wish to consider. With the best will in the world, accidents do happen, horses can be dangerous creatures. Interestingly statistics reveal that you are more likely to be injured on the ground on the yard for example when loading, than you are when riding.

Personal accident cover can either be provided as part of your main equine policy or you can source it separately. Again, organisations such as the BHS provide this as part of their gold membership. And other equine organisations may offer some limited cover, for example, British Riding Clubs "BRC" offer some accident cover to their members but only whilst competing at a BRC event so again, it is essential that you read your policy very carefully and understand its parameters.

Depending on what type of policy you have and how comprehensive it is, costs will vary from around £150 ($235) per year to several hundred pounds/dollars. Equine insurance creates divided opinions amongst many in the horsey community. Some people would not be without it and have as much as they can afford whereas others are much more sceptical, particularly if they have had a previous bad experience with an insurer and may

Chapter 5: Vetting before purchase and insurance

choose instead to make a monthly payment into a savings account to cover vets bills as and when they arise.

Choose your insurer wisely and if necessary one of the best people to offer you sound unbiased advice, is your vet. They are on the sharp end of the claims process as in the event of a claim, your insurance company will be liaising with your veterinary practice to pay invoices and so vets get a pretty good feel for the reputable and professional organisations to deal with and who to avoid. I have known a veterinary practice ask for credit card details before commencing treatment on a horse once they heard who the horse was insured with.

Beware of canvassing opinion on social media as some people do not read their policies carefully and then get caught out through their own omission and not due to any fault on the part of the insurer; without knowing a situation in great detail, it is very hard to make a judgement based on what you may read in a forum or on Facebook.

And finally, make sure your insurance cover in whatever format, commences when money has changed hands and when transfer of ownership of your new Connemara pony has passed to you.

Chapter 6: Bringing your new Connemara pony home

The arrival of a new horse is a very exciting time and it is important that you have all the necessary arrangements in place before your new equine arrives.

If your Connemara pony is going to a livery yard then there will be little for you to do other than to make sure that they have the date of arrival and that you have signed any relevant livery contracts. If your new horse is going to live at home then your shelter and grazing must be ready plus all of the yard equipment you will need to look after your new friend, here is a check list:-

- Fork for mucking out and collecting droppings
- Wheelbarrow
- Broom
- Feed bowl possibly
- Feed if appropriate
- Water buckets or trough
- Grooming kit
- Head collar and lead rope
- Vet box
- Hay supply depending on the time of year but always best to have some hay available at all times

Some of this will be required even if your horse is going to a livery yard, you may not need yard equipment but you will need a head collar, lead rope and a grooming kit.

It is usually good practice to worm your new Connemara pony on arrival then you will know for yourself that the horse is clear. Turning out a horse with an unknown worm burden will only contaminate your pasture and if you are on a livery yard, then

Chapter 6: Bringing your new Connemara home

they will probably insist that the new horse is wormed when it arrives.

If you are arranging insurance cover then make sure this starts from the date ownership transfers so this will include any time in transit; depending on where your Connemara pony is coming from, this could cover potentially a couple of days and injuries can occur when travelling.

Register your new acquisition with a local veterinary practice, ask friends who they recommend or local horsey social media groups will give you some tips.

Check the passport of the horse carefully upon arrival, make sure that it relates to the horse in question by carefully checking the diagrammatic description of your horse's markings and distinguishing features.

It is a legal requirement in the UK that every horse and pony has a valid passport and this requirement was introduced by the European Union in 2005. Usually these are issued by breed societies if the animal is registered to a breed society and has known breeding. Other organisations may issue passports to animals of unknown breeding, these bodies are called PIOs or Passport Issuing Organisations, this document simply records the animal's physical description and year of birth if known. Some bodies that hold breed records will issue passports to animals of

Chapter 6: Bringing your new Connemara home

unknown breeding and record them in a different section of their register, the passport may well be a different colour and these documents are often referred to by their colour.

Your Connemara pony may be micro chipped and if it isn't, it is a good policy to consider this for security reasons. New European Union legislation introduced in 2009 now means that is compulsory for all new foals to be micro chipped in the UK before the owner can apply for a passport. If your Connemara pony is micro chipped then there is usually a sticker on the passport with the unique number, it looks rather like a bar code. You will need to change ownership details with both the Passport Issuing Organisation and the microchip register to declare that you are the new owner.

Another deterrent to theft is the process of freeze marking or branding where the horse is marked with a unique identification number somewhere on his body, usually the neck or the shoulder. There is an organization in the UK called Farmkey who offer this service. This is a visible deterrent to would be thieves and again it is important that you register yourself as the new owner if your new Connemara pony is freeze marked.

Chapter 7: Care of your Connemara

Chapter 7: Care of your Connemara pony

Caring for a horse on a daily basis is not rocket science, there are a number of daily tasks that need to be completed and other routine tasks at more distant intervals. The topics that will be considered in this chapter are:-

- Feeding
- Watering
- Grooming
- First Aid
- Veterinary care
- Farriery

Feeding

It is important to understand first of all, how horses and ponies are designed to eat in the wild. They are peripatetic so they like to roam constantly and they are trickle feeders so they eat little and often. They have a very small stomach, about the size of a rugby ball and a very long hind gut which is designed to process fibre rather than cereals.

Horses were created to graze or eat for around 16 out of every 24 hours with food matter spending only a short time in the stomach and a much longer time in the hind gut where the material is broken down and nutritional elements extracted. A lifestyle and feeding regime that mimics this therefore is considered to be the best and most healthy option for any equine. Horses should always have access to fibre at all times so with a stabled horse this would involve feeding hay ad lib rather than on a ration. It is not possible to over feed hay and your Connemara pony will not get fed up with it but it is possible for a horse to have too much grass.

Chapter 7: Care of your Connemara

Horses should eat hay and grass as the bulk of their diet as that is what their digestive system is designed to process. Feeding hard feed/grain feed/compound feed/straights that is anything other than hay and grass, is quite a specialist business. It is impossible to cover everything about feeding in this book as that would be a book all by itself.

There are some rules of feeding which owners use as a benchmark for good feeding practice and they are as follows:-

- Feed little and often
- Feed plenty of fibre
- Always feed good quality, clean forage
- Ensure that feed receptacles are cleaned out thoroughly after each use and there is no residue or trace of food left
- Feed the best quality food you can afford
- Always feed at the same times, horses thrive on routine
- Ensure that there is always access to a supply of fresh, clean water at feed time
- Leave horses alone with their feed
- Do not make sudden changes to the diet as the microbial population in the hind gut has adapted to break down certain nutrients and you will cause digestive upset if you suddenly introduce a different feed. Introduce new feed gradually over a period of seven to ten days
- Ensure that your hay supply is as consistent as possible; introducing different hay or even hay baled on a different part of a field on a different day when the weather conditions have changed, may cause digestive upset
- Do not work a horse hard after feeding, allow at least an hour to elapse, this includes bringing in horses from pasture who should be allowed to stand in for a while before they are ridden
- Feed something succulent – apples or carrots – particularly through the winter months. Carrots should be sliced lengthways and NOT chopped – a round slice of carrot can become lodged in the oesophagus and lead to choking. Apples should be cored and sliced

Chapter 7: Care of your Connemara

- Always dampen feeds if they do not have any wet element to them such as soaked sugar beet. Some feeds need to be pre-soaked so always check the bag for instructions.

Where possible, horses and ponies are happiest living out rather than being stabled, subject to some exceptions, and therefore a ready supply of grazing will fulfill the majority of the nutritional needs of your Connemara pony. When grazing is poor usually in the winter months, it can be supplemented with hay.

The key source of nutrition for the horse is fibre and hay and grass will provide this. Connemara ponies, because of their size and their ethnicity, are considered to be "good doers" much like other native breeds of pony from the UK and this means that they gain weight quite easily and hold condition well and so should thrive on this food source alone. The only caveat to enter is grazing that is too, lush perhaps in the spring months, as this can cause specific health issues, this will be covered in the next chapter.

You might not think it but there are several different types of hay; seed hay which is a commercially grown hay and meadow hay which comes from old established pasture. Seed hay is a longer, coarser yellow hay and meadow hay is softer and usually greener in colour. There is also a source of fibre called haylage and this differs from hay in that it is baled when the grass is still quite wet and then sealed into plastic. Haylage has a higher moisture and nutritional content than hay and is not usually suitable for feeding to ponies or good doers as the sugar levels are greater although haylage can vary from supplier to supplier. Haylage has the advantage over hay in that it is usually dust free so is a popular choice for horses with respiratory issues but it is not suitable to feed to all animals. There is also another product called horsehage which is similar to haylage. Silage is another product made from grass and contains an even higher moisture level than haylage but this is not suitable as fodder for horses and is generally only fed to cattle.

Chapter 7: Care of your Connemara

Because fibre is so important in the horses' diet, it is important for you as the owner to find a good hay supplier, someone who can provide you with a consistent quality of hay that is cut from good, weed free pasture. Hay can be provided in bales of different sizes and many commercial hay producers prefer to produce large bale hay as it is much easier than making smaller bales. You will need somewhere waterproof to store your hay, preferably a building with good vehicular access. Storing hay outside is a real chore in the winter months as it is almost impossible to keep it dry even using tarpaulins.

Your Connemara pony can be fed hay either from the floor, via a manger at chest height or from a hay net. Many people prefer feeding hay from the floor as this is the natural grazing angle of the horse and it promotes good drainage from the nostrils but this is not always practical and there can be more wastage. The alternatives are to feed from a secure hayrack usually a wooden structure or via a hay net which is literally a net that you fill with hay and then tie up to the wall.

Hay nets can be bought with holes of different sizes; the smaller hole nets are described as haylage nets and these encourage the horse to eat more slowly as it takes him longer to access the contents. Hay nets can be a hazard if they fall down as they can become entangled around the legs of the horse and cause an accident. It is important therefore that they are securely tied up to a metal ring tie on the wall by pulling through the cord and then feeding through the bottom of the net and back up through the metal ring, the net is then secured with a quick release knot on the body of the net and finally flipped over so the knot is at the back. The net must be at head height because as it empties out it will fall down the wall and become lower.

If you are feeding hay on the field to your Connemara pony in order to supplement grazing then hay can either be fed on the ground or via a hay net as in the stable, although your fencing may be too low or not suitable as a securing point in which case you could secure to the field shelter or stable. Some people feeding a lot of horses will use a large round bale brought in on a tractor and this can be placed underneath metal cattle rings which are designed to prevent the hay from being dragged all over the field. If you are feeding hay on the field to more than one horse, it is important to remember that horses can be territorial over feed and you need to provide an additional hay station for the number of horses as there is bound to be one member of the herd that is chased away and not allowed access.

Some horses have respiratory issues which mean that they can react to dust and hay can be dusty. If feeding haylage is not an option in these situations then it is possible to soak or steam hay; this reduces dust and any mould spores which may irritate the horses' airways. Hay can be soaked in a large container filled with clean water, the net can be immersed fully and must be soaked for a period of at least twenty minutes and then hung up to drain. Or soaked hay can be fed loose in a container on the floor. The water in which the hay is soaked MUST be changed at least every 24 hours as it will become toxic, a large plastic or metal container which can be filled via a hosepipe and then drained via a tap near a yard drain is the easiest way to manage this.

Steaming hay is the other option and there are commercially available hay steamers produced by a company called Haygain which are specifically designed for this purpose. It is important to steam the hay evenly and at the correct temperature otherwise you can actually increase mould and contaminant levels so try and resist the temptation of creating some homemade device with a plastic dustbin and a wallpaper steamer which seems to be a popular DIY alternative published on social media!

Some Connemara pony owners, if they are showing or competing, may want to add to this fibre diet in order to promote a "show bloom" but one must be very cautious of over feeding as this can cause serious health issues and also contribute to excitable behaviour which is not ideal if your Connemara pony is under saddle with a small person on board. There may be circumstances when you want or need to feed an additional feed to your horse such as:-

Chapter 7: Care of your Connemara

- You have an elderly horse which is not maintaining weight although you should note that the usual cause for weight loss in older horses is lack of long fibre i.e hay and grass through either inadequate supply or dental issues
- Your horse is doing a lot of work in terms of ridden hours and/or competing
- You have a mare in foal, she will require feeding for the last 3-4 months of the gestation period
- Your horse is recovering from illness or injury

If you wish to feed an additional compound feed or mix to your Connemara pony then take advice from your instructor or trainer who should be able to guide you in the direction of an appropriate supplementary feed. All of the major feed companies in the UK, Saracen, Dengie, Dodson & Horrell, Allen & Page, Blue Chip to name but a few, have nutritional advice lines and they can provide information both over the phone and in person. They can arrange to visit your yard, weigh your Connemara pony and give a condition score and then based on age, type and workload, recommend an appropriate feed from their range.

The only possible thing you may wish to add to a fibre only diet on a routine basis is a broad spectrum mineral and vitamin supplement. Horses being fed mix or hard feed will normally receive an adequate and balanced mineral and vitamin blend as part of their diet. Clearly you cannot see the analysis of your hay and grass which will vary over the seasons in any event so to ensure your Connemara pony is receiving all of the necessary nutrients, then using a broad based mineral and vitamin supplement is a good course of action to follow.

In the UK there is a product available called Fast Fibre made by a company called Allen & Page, it comes in the form of a pellet and is literally hay in a bucket. The nuts only take one minute to soak and this is a very popular feed choice for ponies as it is non heating and not cereal based. Fast Fibre is an excellent option if you need to feed a broad spectrum vitamin and mineral supplement or anything else in powdered form such as antibiotics,

Chapter 7: Care of your Connemara

worming granules or Phenylbutazone which is a non-steroidal anti-inflammatory very commonly used in horses to treat both pain and inflammation.

There are other products similar to Fast Fibre on the market which basically have a very low nutritional level. Some need pre-soaking others do not so for example, fibre nuts and grass nuts which are just as they describe. It would be usual practice to dampen these slightly and also add a chop or chaff to these to stop your Connemara pony bolting the feed.

Some horses are very greedy and will eat feed too quickly so it is normal to add a chop or chaff to help bulk the nuts or pencils and encourage mastication thereby reducing the likelihood of inadequately chewed food arriving in the horse's stomach.

A chop or chaff is usually a mixture of chopped oat or barley straw and hay. There is a real fashion these days to add in lots of extras in order to tempt the horse, in fact these extras are there to tempt the owner and makes something very plain look more appealing. In reality, they are not normally needed and are usually sugar based which is something you would seek to avoid. The most common additive is molasses, which the chop is sprayed with before being bagged hence the name mollichaff or mollichop. It is possible to purchase a plain, dust extracted oat straw, in the UK there is one made by a company called Honeychop. They do lots of fancy types of chop as well but they do have a very plain, clean chop which you can add freely by the handful to slow down a keen feeder.

Watering

All horses and ponies need access to fresh water on a continuous basis, there are many different ways to provide this which are covered in the next chapter. Be aware that water that has been standing for some time whilst it may appear clear, will suffer from taint as it absorbs odours from the surrounding environment so the water will need to be changed at least once every twelve hours even if it appears clean.

Chapter 7: Care of your Connemara

Grooming

Your Connemara pony will need to be groomed on a daily basis, this is a very important time spent with your pony as not only can you check all over the pony's body for any issues or ailments but it is a great bonding opportunity – have you ever seen groups of horses in the field mutually grooming each other?

It is common practice to tie a horse up to a ring tie to which a small continuous loop of baler twine has been added first. The golden rule is tie the hay net to the ring and the horse to the twine. The purpose of this distinction is that you want the hay net to be as secure as possible but you want the twine to break if your Connemara pony panics and pulls back. The horse is tied up using a quick release knot. Most people keep baler twine from their hay bales although if you buy large bale hay this will be net or even plastic wrapped. Beware using twine from the bigger, square Heston bales as this twine is thicker and stronger than that used for small bale hay and will not break so easily.

A basic grooming kit can be purchased from any saddlery and will include the following items:-

- Dandy brush
- Body Brush
- Plastic curry comb
- Metal curry comb
- Rubber curry comb
- Water brush
- Mane comb
- Several sponges of different colours, one for eyes, one for nostrils and one for dock, that's the mucky bit under the tail!
- Stable rubber which is a linen cloth about the size of tea towel
- Hoof pick

The dandy brush is a harder, stiffer brush which tends to be used on thick coats such as winter coats and to remove mud, it can be

Chapter 7: Care of your Connemara

used on any part of your Connemara pony. The body brush is a broader, flatter, softer brush which would be used on a finer coat or after you have removed mud and dirt from your horse with the dandy brush first. The metal curry comb should never be used on the horse itself but is used to clean the body brush after a few strokes across the horse's coat, it removes hair, dust and dirt from the body brush. The plastic and rubber curry combs may be used on the horse's body, the plastic curry comb is particularly useful at removing dried mud in the winter. The rubber curry comb, which is an oval shape, is very good at removing loose hair when the horse is shedding its winter coat in the spring months; you can use this in a circular motion on the horse's body and then lift out all the loose hair which accumulates within the oval spaces.

The body brush may be used on your Connemara pony's mane and tail but if you over brush the main and tail you will cause the hair to break off and become thin and spartan. Don't ever be tempted to use the plastic curry comb on the mane or tail when they are coated in dried mud as you will really damage the hair. It is better to untangle the hair with your fingers and then wash the tail every few days to keep it clean and soft. Applying baby oil or a mane and tail conditioner will help you get through the tangles and obstructions and minimize hair breakage. A human hair brush is always a good option for a thick and unruly mane and a grooming kit would not be complete without a mane comb but use the hairbrush first to make the job easier for the mane comb.

A water brush is a slightly stiff brush that is used to lay the mane and this is essentially dampening the mane and encouraging it to lie on the correct side which is the right hand side of the neck or "the off side". The left hand side of the horse which is the side that horses tend to be led from is called "the near side".

Sponges are used to keep the horses' eyes clean and comfortable and a sponge of a different colour is used in the dock area which is under the tail. Stallions and geldings (neutered male horses) need to have their penis and surrounding area kept clean on a regular basis, this area is called the sheath.

Chapter 7: Care of your Connemara

The usual grooming procedure is to first tie your up your Connemara pony and pick out all four feet into a bucket or skip. Then begin work on the body with either the dandy brush or the body brush depending on which is more appropriate for your horse's coat – start at the top of the neck and work towards the tail. If the horse has a lot of dried mud on the coat then it can be helpful to start with a plastic curry comb to remove the worst of it. Likewise if the horse is shedding coat then use the rubber curry comb first to remove loose hair, this also has a massaging effect on the horse's skin. If you are using a body brush then remember to clean it after every few strokes with the metal curry comb and every so often, knock out the dust in the curry comb onto the floor away from the horse. Work down each leg individually and then move the horse's head collar onto the neck keeping the horse tied up and secure and carefully brush the head and face.

Next brush and lay the mane by dampening it with the water brush. If your horse's mane does not naturally lie on the off or right hand side of the horse's neck then it is possible to train the mane over by dampening it and brushing it across to the correct side and then dividing it into bunches and plaiting each individual bunch down. It takes a few weeks of persistent plaiting to train the mane across but if you want to compete your Connemara pony plaited then you will need to have the plaits on the correct side. And then to the tail, untangle with your fingers and either finger comb or use a very soft brush lightly on the tail hairs to avoid them breaking, baby oil or a spray-in equine conditioner will help. Sponge the eyes with a damp sponge and then use a different sponge for the dock area and sheath. Finally, wipe the horse over with a linen cloth called a stable rubber, this removes dust and leaves a nice shine on the coat.

Even if you don't groom on a daily basis, it is imperative that your Connemara pony's hooves are picked out and checked daily, more frequently if the animal is being ridden.

The majority of the underside of the hoof of a horse "the sole" is insensitive and hard but the central portion, the "V" shape which is called the frog, is soft. The frog acts as a shock absorber and

Chapter 7: Care of your Connemara

aids the return of blood flow back up the leg and this area needs to be avoided when picking out the horse's feet as it is sensitive and you can cause damage to it with the hoof pick. Work with the sharp tip of the hoof pick from the horse's heel down towards the toe, first on one side and then the other removing any stones and mud, avoid the frog. Front feet are fairly easy to pick out but hind feet can be more difficult and some horses will snatch them away, position yourself well to the side of the horse so you don't get kicked. There is a safe way to pick up a hind leg and that is by sliding your hand and arm down and around the inside of the leg and cupping the hoof in your hand. This avoids stretching your arm across the back of the hind leg of the horse whilst it is raised as if the horse kicks out at this point, you could incur a nasty injury.

First Aid

We have already talked about registering your new Connemara pony with a veterinary practice on arrival but you may find that you have to deal with some minor issues yourself as the weeks go by. Most horse owners become quite skilled at dealing with wounds and other problems, it is expensive calling the vet out and the trick is to know when to call the vet and when you can manage yourself. Vets have a standard call out charge but this will increase quite significantly if you need to consult your vet out of hours which is classified as evenings and weekends, it may well be double the standard call out charge or even more.

Minor injuries and issues can be dealt with by most owners, as your skills increase so will the size of your vet box! Some veterinary practices run courses for horse owners, first aid is a popular topic. A competent horse owner or an experienced friend can show you how to manage most low key situations such as a cut or wound but if in doubt, always take professional advice. A basic veterinary box could include the following items:-

- Several rolls of vet wrap which is a self-adhesive bandage

Chapter 7: Care of your Connemara

- A large roll of gauze covered wadding which can be used as a dressing or padding or wipes/ pads to clean wounds, this can be cut to size
- Cotton Wool
- Electricians tape, several rolls, used to secure bandages and dressings
- Duct tape, a broad waterproof tape used to cover dressings on limbs in wet conditions
- A thermometer
- A sharp pair of scissors
- Curved end scissors also called fetlock scissors
- Hibiscrub which is an anti-bacterial solution for cleaning wounds
- Iodine spray
- Metal bowl for use in cleaning wounds
- Veterinary poultice such as Animalintex which is designed to be applied to a wound or issue such as a hoof abscess and draw out infection, again can be cut to size
- Wound gel such as Intrasite or an alternative
- Fly repellant

Veterinary Care

The ideal with vets is to see them as little as possible. However, your Connemara pony will need to at least have its teeth checked annually and also be vaccinated against equine influenza and tetanus. This is a combined vaccination usually administered into the neck of the horse. The anti-tetanus element is given biennially so every other year, the vaccinations will be recorded on your Connemara pony's passport. Apart from good practice, you may find that you cannot compete at certain equine events if your horse does not have this vaccination cover.

Vets often check horses teeth at vaccination time although some young horses (where the mouth is still developing) and older horses that are beginning to encounter dental issues, will need their teeth checked more frequently. A horse can be aged by its

Chapter 7: Care of your Connemara

teeth with a reasonable degree of accuracy up to the age of six, after that it becomes more difficult to age as the horse gets older.

Your Connemara pony's teeth will erupt continuously throughout its life hence the need for the pony to always be grinding long fibre such as hay or grass. The flat grinding surfaces of the teeth are called tables and the large molars at the back can develop sharp hooks as they grind against each other and it is the presence of these amongst other things that the vet is checking for. Sharp hooks will press into the flesh inside the horse's mouth and cause sores and ulceration and become extremely painful.

The vet will check the mouth of the your Connemara pony by fitting what is called a Hausmans gag which is a metal device which holds the pony's mouth open so that the teeth can be examined in safety. If there are any sharp hooks present then the vet can remove these with a metal file which is called a rasp which has a roughened edge for this purpose, some vets use electric equipment to do the same job. It sounds pretty grizzly when a horse is having its teeth rasped but it really doesn't hurt. Despite this, some horses are not keen on this procedure and will require a degree of sedation which your vet can administer before he starts work.

Your Connemara pony will also need to be wormed against a range of parasites at regular intervals and your vet can advise you of an appropriate worming programme for your animal. The usual worming intervals are 6-8 weeks. You may also be offered FECs by your practice, this stands for Faecal Egg Counts which is a method of checking from a sample of your horse's droppings what the worm burden is for your particular horse, this can provide guidance on how frequently you should worm. Faecal Egg Counts do not detect all worms so even if the worm count for your Connemara pony is low or within acceptable parameters, there will still be a need to worm against other types of parasite such as encysted red worm and tapeworm, neither of which will show up on an egg count. In the UK, there is now a new test taken from the saliva in the horse's mouth which can test for the presence of tapeworm.

Chapter 7: Care of your Connemara

It is important when you worm your Connemara pony that you use wormers from one chemical grouping and do not keep alternating the brand each time, again your vet can advise you. Worms and parasites are developing strong resistance to these drugs through their systematic overuse. Wormers may be administered to the horse either by a plastic syringe into the side of the horse's mouth where he has no teeth or by adding granules to the feed. Get an experienced friend or your vet to show you how to do it the first couple of times, some horses are very resistant to being wormed and will put up quite a fight.

If you keep your Connemara pony at home and are conscientious about clearing droppings from the pasture, you may find that regular worm counts say every three months, reveal that the parasite burden is so low that you do not need to worm your pony at that time. But even with low FEC you will need still to worm for tapeworm in the spring and autumn and for encysted red worm in the winter, neither of which will show up on a FEC.

At the other end of the veterinary spectrum, there are the emergency situations and there are three possible occasions which constitute an emergency and at which point you should reach for your phone to call your vet before doing anything else and they are:-

- Colic, abdominal pain, even a hint of this needs prompt veterinary intervention as it is life threatening and time is of the essence. Even if your vet monitors by phone because it is just a mild case, it is essential that they are aware you have a potential colic as the situation can change rapidly
- Uncontrollable bleeding such as a severed artery
- Injury to a joint. However tiny the injury such as a puncture wound, these are life threatening once infection has entered the joint capsule. An injury to a joint will require immediate hospitalization so that the wound can be flushed in sterile conditions

Chapter 7: Care of your Connemara

If you don't have your own transport then you should always keep handy the phone numbers of friends or transport companies who can move your Connemara pony to an equine hospital in an emergency.

Farriery

Your Connemara pony will need to see a farrier on a regular basis throughout the year. Horses' hooves grow continuously and need checking and trimming by a qualified professional on a 6 to 8 week basis. If your horse is shod then the frequency of attention may increase slightly.

Your farrier will trim your Connemara pony's hooves to maintain shape, cut away any ragged areas from both the wall and the frog which is the "V" shaped central part of the sole of the hoof, re-balance the foot and generally check for any health issues. Farriers are not the only people who are qualified to care for horses' feet; there are a group of people who advocate not shoeing the horse at all and leaving it "barefoot" and their horses are cared for by people called podiatrists. However, a lot of people who use farriers do not have shod horses and their horses are just trimmed regularly, it is the same difference.

It is clearly easier and cheaper not to shoe the horse but some horses need shoeing either because they are working or because they need to wear what are called remedial shoes. For example, horses and ponies that suffer from laminitis are offered support when they are lame from glue on shoes and frog pads, this is an essential part of rehabilitation and the role of the farrier in helping to care for a laminitic horse is absolutely key.

The basic horse shoe is called a hunter shoe but some horses wear shoes which differ from the conventional shape to support feet that have conformational defects such as low/collapsed or what are called underrun heels which can contribute to certain kinds of lameness. Some horses wear pads to protect flat soles, the underside of the foot, competition horses will wear shoes that are fullered which is a groove running around the ground bearing surface of the shoe to promote grip. And farriers will add stud holes to some shoes so that competition horses can be fitted with different types of stud to promote grip and balance when turning at speed, narrow more pointed studs when the ground is hard and dry and fatter studs when it is wet and slippery. There are many, many types of horse shoe in terms of shape and material (stainless steel, aluminum, plastic) and people spend a lifetime learning about them.

Many people will call the farrier in the first instance if their horse goes lame, following the old adage of "99% of lameness is in the foot", he or she can be a good place to start any investigation. For example, if your Connemara pony has a hoof abscess, a farrier would easily be able to deal with this and resolve it without recourse to the vet. For more complex issues however, you would need to make contact with your veterinary practice.

The only real way to influence the quality of the horn of the hoof is by nutrition hence the requirement for a balanced diet and possible vitamin and mineral supplementation, particularly Biotin, which is a Vitamin from the B Group Complex and which is necessary for good horn structure. Your farrier can advise you of an appropriate supplement if you should need it for your Connemara pony or any other additions to your vet box to promote good hoof care. Remember the old saying, "no foot no horse".

Chapter 8: Grassland and Stabling

As discussed in a previous chapter, the best way to keep your Connemara pony is in as natural way as possible, mimicking the lifestyle that the pony would have in the wild which is to roam and graze, eating little and often within a herd. Horses are very sociable creatures and are happiest kept in a group with their own kind. If the prospect of having more than one does not fill you with enthusiasm, it is possible to offer them the companionship of a different species such as a donkey or even sheep or goats. The difficulty with keeping two horses or ponies is that they will pair bond and can then become difficult to separate if that is the plan.

Grassland

The rule of thumb is that each equine needs an acre of grazing land to sustain it. With a good doer like a Connemara pony, an acre is ample but horses are picky grazers and so it is always best to section off the land into parcels. This allows you to preserve pasture against over grazing or the ravages of the winter months when the land becomes poached in wet weather and it will also then allow you to control grass intake in the growing months when too much spring grass can cause health issues. An acre of land per horse or pony will give you the opportunity to do this.

Laminitis

Horses and ponies can suffer from a disease called laminitis which is often, although not always, related to grazing.

Laminitis is named after the laminae which are tissues found within the hoof capsule; there are sensitive and insensitive laminae which interleave together and act as structural supports to the bone in the foot called the pedal bone. If your Connemara pony has too much sugar in its diet which can come from any source – grass, hay or hard feed - then the sensitive laminae in the hooves, usually the front feet, become engorged with blood, inflammed and painful and your pony will become very lame with a strong digital pulse. The digital pulse is when you can feel the blood flowing through the artery going into the hooves. If there is inflammation in the hoof or hooves then the blood flow is restricted and essentially backs up into the artery, meaning that there is a discernible pulse much like the pulse you can feel in your own wrist. The stronger the pulse, the more inflammation there will be in the hoof. Faint digital pulses are normal and there is always some variation from horse to horse so you should learn to feel what is normal for your pony so that you can spot any differences.

One of the main causes of laminitis is too much sugar within the grass, particularly at growing times of year such as the spring when the grass is rich but also in the autumn when there are cold nights and sunny days, this can cause a surge of fructans within the grass, potentially harmful to the horse. The golden rule with stabled horses in the winter months is to never turn them out onto frosty grazing, wait until it has melted completely and then turn them out. This is because the grass closes down in the frosty weather and then as it melts, a sugar spike or surge is created, potentially harmful to vulnerable horses.

Some breeds of horse and pony are more susceptible to laminitis than others. Generally, native ponies are considered to be more at risk genetically and because they are good doers who have evolved to live off very little. Your Connemara pony will be at risk from this disease because of its native ancestry. So the ability to restrict grazing at certain times of year by sectioning areas off is very useful.

Horses and ponies suffering from laminitis should be kept on a strict fibre based diet only so absolutely no cereals and hay that has been soaked for at least twenty minutes preferably longer as this reduces the naturally occurring sugar content. Once an episode of laminitis has been controlled, going forward it is considered best practice to keep horses and ponies on as much fibre as possible and restrict any hard feed to products that contain a naturally occurring sugar level of less than ten percent. It is not possible to analyse grass on a daily basis and the nutritional value must vary so much from week to week throughout the seasons but we can control the horse's other food sources such as the hay that is fed and the amount of ration or hard feed.

You can find more information about laminitis from the Laminitis Trust who are an orgnisation dedicated to research into this disease and who also support owners acting as a reference point for those seeking help and advice. Laminitis is a painful and nasty disease and once a horse has had it, they are more at risk of the disease reoccurring. Your vet can advise you further if you have any concerns but prevention is always better than cure.

Fencing

The land on which you graze your Connemara pony must be adequately fenced, there are a number of different ways to do this:-

- Post and rail, the most expensive between £10-£15 per metre ($15-$25)
- Electric tape probably the least expensive £2-£5 per metre ($3-$8)
- Post and high tensile wire
- Post and stock netting

Whichever materials you choose, the fencing must be safe and secure, it should keep your Connemara pony in and also any other stock you may choose to graze alongside – clearly, post and rail for example would be of no use if you wished to graze some sheep with your pony.

Electric fencing is a good, cheaper alternative to post and rail and is much more flexible, particularly when it comes to sectioning off different areas. Some people post and rail the perimeter of an

Chapter 8: Grassland and Stabling

area and then subdivide within that area with electric tape and fibreglass or plastic posts.

The key with electric fencing is to present a good, solid line to the horse rather than something flimsy or insubstantial because once your Connemara pony has learned to disrespect the fencing, you are likely to suffer from escapes and injuries. The fence is attached to a battery, usually something similar to a car battery, and an energizer creates a pulse so the electrical current is not continuous. You need to have a sufficient level of voltage to deter horses from trying to escape as clearly loose horses are undesirable and horses can also become quite badly injured if they become entangled in the electric tape.

There are different types of tape available usually in the colours white or green, there is also something called turbo rope which is exactly that, a white rope. These all have metal strands contained within them. It is the metal which conducts the electricity and it is the metal which can cause nasty injuries if the horse becomes entangled.

The main issue to remember is that you will need to adjust recommended fence heights to suit the size of your Connemara pony; the bottom line of tape or rail must be low enough to prevent escape but not so low that there is a risk of injury to the pony.

Shelter

All horses and ponies that live out i.e. are grazing outside 24 hours a day year round, need access to shelter. This is just as important in the summer – to offer respite from the sun, heat and the flies – as in the winter, to provide shelter from the wind and rain.

Shelter can be provided for your Connemara pony in the form of a stable which is left permanently open and available to the pony or a field shelter which is basically a three side structure with an area of the front in filled to act as a wind break.

If you are grazing more than one horse, you need to make sure that the shelter you use will adequately accommodate all of the horses, bearing in mind the hierarchy in the herd and that some horses like more space than others; some very dominant horses can prevent others from coming into the shelter. Whatever you choose, you will need to provide some form of bedding in the base of the building not necessarily because the horse will lie down as horses will quite happily lie down out in the open but because the ground will become poached in the winter months. Site the shelter with the back of it towards the prevailing winds.

Watering arrangements

All horses require fresh water to be continuously available.

A safe trough in the field with water piped to it is one of the best means to provide this but can have the drawback of freezing up in the winter, so one of your daily jobs is to check the water and keep it clear and free flowing. If there is a risk of burst pipes during the winter months then the trough can be disconnected during this time and an alternative mechanism of providing water used. One of the other difficulties with a self-filling trough is that it is not possible to monitor how much your Connemara pony is drinking, which can be a clue to ill health or other issues.

Chapter 8: Grassland and Stabling

Water may be provided via buckets but this can be laborious depending on the location of the water supply. If the water supply is distant then run a hose from it to the field, this will allow you to easily change the water and keep it topped up. In the winter, the hose will freeze so keep a second hosepipe on a reel inside the house and unroll this every morning to run water to the field, removing it in the evening as any droplets of water contained within the run will freeze up overnight and render the hose useless the next day.

If you are going to use a trough, make sure that it is designed for stock i.e. there are no sharp edges on which the pony could catch itself. Old metal baths are not suitable because of the sharp edges.

Land management

Whether your Connemara pony is living out or only at grass for part of the day, it is important to check your land daily. A walk round will offer you a good look at the fencing to make sure it is intact, an opportunity to remove any rubbish or foreign objects and an inspection of the water supply.

It is also necessary to remove the droppings from the field, preferably on a daily basis but certainly weekly. Horses will not graze land that is contaminated with manure so removing droppings will help preserve the integrity of the pasture and is also essential as part of your programme of worm control.

Rotation of the grazing, which means dividing up the area into sections and resting some whilst grazing others, will help you preserve the quality of both the grass and the land it grows upon by allowing pasture to rest.

Resting pasture gives you an opportunity to treat for weeds, either through spraying or manual removal, and also to harrow the land and fertilize as necessary, sewing grass in the bald areas. A soil sample will reveal if the pH. balance of the soil is at the optimum level for good grass growth and this level should ideally be 6.5. A pH reading that is not around the desired level will mean that grass will not thrive as efficiently, as this will in turn allow the

Chapter 8: Grassland and Stabling

incursion of other plants which may not be desirable. It is also possible to have a sample of the herbage analysed in addition to the soil.

Horses are picky feeders and do not graze evenly, leading to the creation of what are called "roughs" and "lawns", the clue is in the description really. We have all seen pasture that has been over grazed - little grass, bald patches and weed predation – and so by resting pasture, you will give the grazing an opportunity to recover and allow time to treat it for weeds and other undesirable plants. Some plants are poisonous to horses and so you need to learn them and how to identify them, below are listed some of the major culprits but this is by no means an exhaustive list.

- Ragwort, has a yellow flower
- Acorns
- Yew
- Laurel
- Horse radish
- Deadly nightshade
- Boxwood
- Foxglove
- Ivy
- Privet
- Lupins

Chapter 9: Exercise and ridden work

Horses do not have to be ridden and many are not for a variety of reasons, too young, too old or retired through illness or injury at any age. The majority of horses begin a ridden career at around the age of four years old, although this is not a hard and fast rule; some are started earlier and then turned away again for a year to mature whilst others are started a bit later if they are still growing and immature, often an issue with big horses. In fact, a horse may be broken in at any age. Sometimes mares that have been used for breeding may be broken in as late as ten years old. Some people seem to think that you can just buy a pony, bring it home and start riding it. Unfortunately that cannot be further from the truth. You cannot learn to ride or what to do from a book so this won't be covered in detail in this book. However, important issues about how the horse is educated to become a riding horse will be discussed.

Early Education

Although a horse's ridden career may not commence until he is four years old, there is a lot of education and handling that should occur whilst the horse is growing and developing. From when the foal is first born, he should be handled right from the outset, fitted with a foal slip which is a tiny head collar, taught to lead and have his feet picked up in preparation for the farrier later. Some people "show" their youngstock by entering them in special classes designed for young horses at shows and there is a lot to be said for getting them out and about, either as a foal at foot so with the mare before weaning or, in yearling classes. But beware over doing this as the foal is still growing and you will cause damage that will manifest itself later on if you put undue stress on developing limbs and joints. Showing youngstock allows them to see the sights and sounds of the showground at a formative age, which can make it much easier if you plan to compete them once they are broken to ride later on.

Chapter 9: Exercise and ridden work

Breaking in or backing

"Breaking in" or being "broken to ride" are both phrases that have rather unpleasant connotations and it is true to say that breaking in did use to be a pretty rough and inhumane experience for the horse. These days one would like to think that humanity has prevailed and that methods are kinder and more educated. Backing (which is perhaps a nicer term) means the same thing. Before a horse is backed, it first has to be "mouthed" which means to be introduced to a bit in its mouth. First bits or starter bits as they are called are often plastic or made of sweet metals to encourage the horse to "mouth" on it, essentially to salivate and play with the bit which encourages a soft mouth. This is usually just done in the stable over a period of several days to allow the horse to get used to it. Following acceptance of the bit, the horse can then be lunged and long reined.

Lungeing

Lungeing is when the horse works around the handler on circles of varying degrees in size, this can be done with or without a saddle (a roller can be used in place of a saddle) and can also be done with or without a rider. Horses may also be lunged over jumps although this takes some degree of skill. Lunge lessons on an experienced horse are also a marvellous way for a rider to concentrate on their position and make improvements without having to worry too much about controlling the horse as well. This is a list of the equipment that you will need.

1. A lunge line, which is a long webbing line with a swivel clip at the end

2. A lunge cavesson, which is a leather sliphead with a thick padded cavesson noseband and several metal rings attached to the front of it from where you will clip the lunge line

3. A lunge whip, which is long handled whip with a long lash

4. A roller or saddle. A roller is a wide, padded, circular piece of webbing which goes around the body of the horse where the girth

Chapter 9: Exercise and ridden work

on a saddled horse would sit. It has metal rings attached on either side to facilitate the fitting of side reins or other training devices

5. Side reins which can be leather or webbing with or without elasticated inserts, there are many different types available. There are lots of other training aids which can be used in place of side reins but it is not the place to examine these options here and it is always best to take professional advice from a trainer before using any of these devices or you can cause undue strain even damage to the horse's musculature.

6. Boots or bandages. It would be usual practice to protect the horse's limbs with different types of boots, brushing boots, tendon boots, overreach boots, these all perform a slightly different function. It is normal to "boot up" all four legs on any horse for lungeing as without the presence of the rider, horses may become quite exuberant and the boots are designed to prevent injury, even more so with a young horse. The other option is to use exercise bandages which provide more support but less protection

Protecting the legs

Thought must be given to protecting the horse's limbs from injury at all times but particularly when the horse is young and being introduced to ridden work. The horse needs to learn to wear a variety of different things on his legs including:-

- Brushing boots
- Tendon boots
- Overreach boots
- Knee Boots
- Hock Boots
- Travelling boots
- Exercise bandages
- Stable Bandages

Chapter 9: Exercise and ridden work

All of these items perform a different function and the horse can be introduced to these before backing, another box ticked if you like.

Brushing boots are boots that are padded on the inside, they tend to be worn in pairs, so fronts or hinds, or all round, so all four legs. They secure on the outside of the horse's legs with either Velcro straps or buckles. They aim to protect the inside of the horse's lower leg below the knee and are so called because some horses with less than good conformation, actually do brush their legs together, usually the hind limbs rather than the front. Tendon boots are very similar other than that they are worn on the front legs only. The padding is down the back of the limb below the knee rather than the side and they tend to be an open fronted boot with straps that go across the front of the horse's leg. These are particularly used on jumping horses that could strike into the back of the front leg with a hind leg; the boots are designed to protect the delicate tendons and ligaments that run down the back of each limb, hence their name. Overreach boots are small plastic or neoprene round boots sometimes called bell boots which fit over the top of the hoof on top of the horse's coronet which is essentially where the hair meets the hoof. Like tendon boots they are designed to protect the back of the hoof from being struck into by a hind leg and so are generally only worn on the front feet.

An alternative to boots are exercise bandages. They offer the horse far less in the way of protection but offer more support to the soft tissues than a boot would. A bandage should only ever be applied to the horse's leg with appropriate padding underneath. A poorly applied bandage as well as being highly dangerous because it may become loose, can cause pressure points on the soft tissues and may actually damage the very structures it is intended to protect.

Whether to use boots or bandages when the horse is working is usually dictated to some extent by what the horse is going to be doing. For example, if the horse is doing dressage and working on an artificial surface then exercise bandages may be an appropriate choice. If he is going hacking and it is a cold and frosty morning,

Chapter 9: Exercise and ridden work

then brushing boots all round would be a better option. Some of the competitive disciplines restrict the equipment that a horse can wear for example, dressage horses must compete with no protection to the lower limb; although you can warm up with either boots or bandages on the horse, they must be removed before the horse enters the competition arena.

Stable bandages, hock boots and to some extent knee boots are all used for protection and support whilst in the stable or travelling. Stable bandages may be used to support the horse during illness or injury and with a slight adjustment, can also be used when travelling. Hock boots can be used whilst travelling and knee boots often called "skeleton knee boots" can be used whilst travelling in conjunction with bandages or they can be used whilst hacking. The other option to bandages and knee/hock boots whilst travelling are travel boots which are long, quite stiff structures shaped and designed to protect the majority of the lower limb from the knee/hock down. It is usually a matter of personal preference as to which system is opted for.

Lungeing the young horse

Lungeing a horse is something that needs to be learned by the handler, it is a skill in its own right and certainly one would want an experienced trainer when starting a young or "green" horse on the lunge - green simply means inexperienced. It is considered best practice to wear a hat and gloves when lungeing. Unlike riding gloves, which should offer some grip on the palm, gloves for lungeing should be made of smooth leather to allow the lunge line to slide through your hand as the horse moves away from you.

Lungeing the young horse is an excellent way of introducing voice commands and the concept of the stick, not as a form of punishment but as a means by which the horse must go forward – later the rider's legs will do this. Using a roller is also excellent preparation for the next stage which is the introduction of the saddle: getting the horse used to something that fits snugly around the torso. It is worth saying that lungeing is not just essential for the young horse before backing, horses benefit from this form of exercise and training throughout their entire lives. It is a great way of exercising the horse if you are short of time or saving a possible fall by popping a fresh horse out on the lunge before you get on but take note, it can make the horse fit so don't do too much before backing otherwise you can find yourself having to get on a fit horse for the first time in its life, better that they are half fit and not feeling quite so full of life!

Long reining

Long reining is similar to lungeing and allows you to work the horse more easily in straight lines in front of you. A horse that is lungeing well can be introduced to the concept of long reining as a logical next step – long reining is rather like lungeing but with two lines, one either side of the horse attaching to each bit ring and feeding through to both hands of the trainer. Once the horse is happy with the concept of long reining in an enclosed environment then he can be taken out around the farm, working forward from the voice to the contact in his mouth via the bit, all excellent preparation for what is to come. There are many benefits to long reining a young horse, some of which are listed below:-

- It teaches the horse to be confident and to go forward on his own
- You can teach the horse to turn left and right and to stop and move forward without any rider which is hugely helpful once the horse has been backed and is riding away
- The horse will get used to the feeling of working forward into the contact which is a different experience to working on the lunge where the horse is essentially opposite rather than in front of the trainer
- The horse can be asked to work in and out of obstacles and to work over and past objects that it may find unknown or frightening

Chapter 9: Exercise and ridden work

Lunging and long reining are quite specialist and would require an experienced and competent trainer, they are not something to be undertaken by a novice or inexperienced person.

Backing

For backing purposes, it would be usual for two people to back the horse. Initially you have a trainer who will lunge and long rein the horse often with the assistant standing at the horse's head, later that assistant will become the rider. In general terms, most people either send their horses away to a professional yard to be backed or have someone come to them if they are competent and just need a second pair of hands. Backing can be quite challenging particularly with little ponies as it can be difficult to find a small but sufficiently competent and lightweight person. With very tiny ponies, it is possible to use a doll or mannequin or an old hessian sack stuffed with straw to mimic a rider – this is also an old trick for horses of any size that are proving themselves to be very difficult to back and before a real rider gets on board.

Once the horse is lungeing and long reining well and is happily travelling forward and understands voice commands then it is time to introduce the saddle. If the horse has been wearing a roller, this isn't usually too challenging a process. As with the roller, the saddle is usually introduced within the confines of the stable for short periods of time, starting with the girth quite loose and then gradually increasing the tension. Once the horse is comfortable wearing the saddle, he can work in it on the lunge and when long reined. It is also good preparation to leave the stirrups down so they bang against his sides, this can cause surprise at first but is a good introduction to the concept of the rider's legs.

The next stage is to introduce the rider, firstly by leaning over the saddle so that the horse can feel the weight of a person with the help of the assistant and then gradually swinging their right leg over so the horse has a leg either side, finally sitting astride and sitting up. Horses' eyes are on the side of their heads so they have 360 degree vision, they can therefore see you in profile when you are on their backs. For a prey animal, this can take some getting used to! Once the horse is happily accepting the rider getting on and off and sitting astride on his back, he can then be led in hand by the trainer, responding to voice commands. This is developed to moving the horse out onto the circle and lungeing him with the rider and then finally removing the lunge line and allowing the horse to be ridden free in the training area. The whole backing process takes about 6 weeks depending on the individual animal.

Riding Away

Riding away is the term used to refer to a horse that has just been backed and is ready to continue its education. In many respects, riding away is often more difficult than backing, as this is when the real education starts and with it, behavioural issues. This is when the horse is taught to walk, trot and canter, move upwards and downwards through the gaits in an obedient fashion, when the concept of contact and outline is introduced and also early hacking in company and roadwork, although hopefully time spent long reining him around the lanes will help in this regard. Riding away is therefore not a job for a novice as the horse needs firm, clear guidance from an educated rider otherwise he will become confused, naughty and then potentially dangerous.

Many people back their horses, do some early riding away and then turn the horse away into the field for a few weeks before bringing them back and carrying on with the horse's education. This allows them some time to take in the new developments in their life. It is worth saying that being able to take your time with a young horse will pay dividends later on and that all the early handling and education builds an important rapport and bond which will be taken through to the work under saddle.

Riding Equipment

Both you and your horse will need the following items:-

Chapter 9: Exercise and ridden work

The Rider

- A correctly fitting safety hat compliant with the current standards
- A selection of warm, short coats – long coats can catch on the back of the saddle whilst you are riding
- Jodhpurs which are a close fitting riding trouser designed to maximize comfort, they are usually partially elasticated for ease of movement
- Long or short boots with a flat, smooth sole and small heel. The requirement for a smooth sole and small heel is so that your foot cannot become caught in the stirrup iron should you fall. A sole with ridges or grooves for grip such as you might find on a pair of yard boots could trap your foot in the stirrup. A lack of heel may mean that your foot could slide right through and trap you. If you ride in short boots then it is possible to combine with these a pair of leather or suede gaiters often called chaps
- Gloves, with grip for riding and with a smooth palm for lungeing, as you will want the lunge line to slide easily through your hands unlike the reins when riding the horse
- Whips or riding crops. Generally the shorter sticks are carried for jumping and the longing sticks or schooling whips for flatwork

The Horse

- A saddle. For leisure riding, what is described as a GP or General Purpose saddle is quite sufficient. There are many other types of saddle for different aspects or disciplines of riding – dressage, show jumping, cross country, racing, endurance riding, Western riding and even side saddle. Fitting saddles is quite an expert process and it would be usual to take advice from a qualified saddle fitter. Ill-fitting saddles cause discomfort to the horse, prevent him from moving and working correctly and can ultimately cause pain and possibly behavioural issues hence the requirement for expert help when choosing and fitting a saddle

Chapter 9: Exercise and ridden work

- A Bridle. Usually available in three sizes, pony, cob and full size. There are many different options available when it comes to choosing nosebands and bits
- Lungeing equipment – lunge line, lunge cavesson, side reins and a roller. So useful to have around the yard. In addition to lungeing for exercise, a lunge line is useful if you have a difficult loader or if you have a lame horse that needs presenting to the vet
- Protective boots and bandages. This depends very much on what the horse is doing in its work, some are designed more for flat work and others for jumping and faster work

Horses do not have to be ridden and many are not because they are too young or too old or retired for some other reason. But horses enjoy regular human contact and handling them and grooming them can create just as special a bond as riding them. Old/retired horses and youngsters can be shown in hand and this can be great occupation and education for an animal that cannot be ridden. Leisure horses in ridden work can be exercised from once a week to almost daily. The work the horse does must reflect his level of fitness and feeding regime otherwise injury and distress can be caused. There is also a thriving competition scene for those who want to get involved in horse sport but horses in competition is the subject of another publication.

Chapter 10: Routines – daily, weekly, monthly

Looking after horses is not just a job, but a way of life. Horses involve daily input from you even if you are not riding them and so it is not a commitment to be undertaken lightly. Here are some of the tasks you will have to do on a daily basis depending on how you keep your Connemara pony.

Daily tasks

- If your Connemara pony is stabled, you will need to properly muck out the stable once a day
- Skip out. This is the removal of droppings only rather than a full muck out and is usually done at feed/hay times.
- Sweep the yard at least once a day
- Maintain and organize your muck heap
- Collect droppings from the field, this may be instead of mucking out if your Connemara pony lives out or it may be in addition to yard work if the horse is only turned out for a proportion of the day
- Groom your Connemara pony
- Pick out the feet at least once a day more frequently if riding the horse or turning the horse out to grass/bringing in from grass
- Prepare feeds as appropriate
- Keep the feed room swept and tidy, old feed on the floor will encourage vermin
- Provide hay if your Connemara pony is stabled or if the grazing is poor due to the time of year
- If you ride, you should clean your tack after it has been used. This promotes the life of the saddlery by taking good care of it and allows you to check for any defects or damage which could potentially put you or your horse's safety at risk

Chapter 10: Routines - daily, weekly, monthly

- Depending on the time of year, your Connemara pony may need a rug, turnout rugs for the field and stable rugs for when the horse is in

Weekly tasks

- Check fencing and field safety by walking around the entire perimeter of the grazing, you should be able to notice any other issues in the main grazing area when you collect the droppings
- Level or rake the school surface if you have one

Summer tasks

- Make good any stable repairs whilst the horse is out during the summer months, treat any wood with wood preservative ahead of the winter
- Spring clean the boxes, removing any cobwebs and dust
- Clean and re-proof all the horse's rugs and store away somewhere dry and rodent free for the winter

Appointments

Use a diary or wall planner to keep track of appointments for your Connmara pony and key dates that you must not forget.

- Diarise your pony's vaccination date and then put an entry in a month prior to remind you to call and make the appointment in plenty of time. If your vaccinations expire then you will need to start the whole course again even if you are one day out. This can affect horses that are competing, as there are complicated rules that can govern vaccination cover for certain competitions. In the UK, many riding organisations borrow the rules laid down by the Jockey Club for vaccination protocol
- Put entries in your diary or planner for the times to worm your pony or do worm counts
- Put in appointments for farrier, physiotherapist or chiropractor. When you have had an appointment, book

Chapter 10: Routines - daily, weekly, monthly

the next one in so that the correct intervals between sessions are maintained

You could do worse than follow the method that farmers employ by working a season ahead so for example in the depths of winter when you are resting grazing, plan ahead for the spring and when you will top or treat the paddocks depending on the weather. In the summer when your pony is out to grass, renovate and repair the stables for the winter months, clear out and do any maintenance work to your hay barn. There is always something to do!

Chapter 11: Minor Ailments

Chapter 11: Minor Ailments

Before looking at some of the more common issues that you may have to deal with as a horse owner, it is worth outlining in general terms some of the key points to look out for and which might indicate that your Connemara pony is unwell:-

- The horse is dull and disinterested
- The horse is not responding in the usual way to daily events and occurrences
- The horse is lying down more than usual or not lying down at all
- The horse is sweating at rest and appears agitated and restless
- A flat, dull coat which is described as "starring"
- Discharge coming from one or both nostrils
- Coughing
- Dull, glazed eyes, any cloudiness to the eye or discharge
- The mucous membranes – the membranes inside the nostrils, the mouth and around the eyes should be salmon pink
- The horse should be eating normally
- Water consumption should be normal, intake will vary according to exercise and to temperature to some extent
- Droppings can vary depending on diet and turnout and the time of year but note any changes to the usual quantity or type without any underlying reason i.e. change of diet or hay
- Urine should be pale yellow in colour, concern should be raised if there is any cloudiness or blood in the urine which may make it appear orange or if the horse is struggling to urinate or "stale"
- A raised temperature, usual level should be 38 degrees

- Elevated respiratory rate. For an adult horse at rest, this should be anywhere between 8-15 breaths per minute
- Increased pulse. The resting pulse rate in an adult horse should be between 36 and 42 beats per minute
- Resting a limb. It is common to rest a hind limb but you would not normally expect the horse to be resting a forelimb
- Pain, heat or swelling to any of the limbs

A good horse owner will be observant and familiar with what is normal for their animal and can therefore quickly spot any changes or differences which might indicate illness or injury. It is worth taking your Connemara pony's temperature, pulse and respiration "TPR" every day for a week at the same time of day so that you have a benchmark for your horse that you can refer to if you have any cause for concern.

The horse as a species can suffer from many different diseases and conditions, this book cannot possibly hope to cover even a fraction of these but it is helpful to consider some of the more common problems that you may come across during the course of horse ownership.

1. Injuries and wounds
2. Respiratory issues
3. Colic
4. Lameness
5. Fly/insect predation

Injuries and wounds

It is inevitable that at some point, you will need to deal with a small injury to your Connemara pony – a cut, bruise or knock or an abscess in the hoof which can all happen irrespective of the best stable management practices.

Chapter 11: Minor Ailments

Injuries and wounds
Sometimes your Connemara pony can injure itself whilst in the field or when being ridden or in competition, horses can even injure themselves in the stable which is why it is important to make sure that the stable is always free of unnecessary equipment or fittings if at all possible and that what is present, is safe for your horse.

Cuts and small wounds are pretty simple to treat. First you will need to clean the wound. Clip or cut away any hair so that you can see what you are dealing with and then clean the wound either under cold running water or using a solution of water and an agent such as Hibiscrub in a bowl. If the wound is several hours old then you will really need to give it a good and thorough clean and if it bleeds again, that is actually a good sign.

Once you have cleaned the wound then you need to decide what you are going to do with it. If you think it is several hours old and it has had mud and dirt in it then your best option is to apply a poultice such as Animalintex. You can use Animalintex both hot and cold but only hot for 48 hours, although you can continue poulticing after that time but the poultice must be dry.

Cut a square of the poultice to accommodate the wound size, apply wet or dry as required and then cover with wadding and either vet wrap or a stable bandage. This dressing needs to be checked and changed every 12 hours. Do not keep re-cleaning the wound, as you will inhibit the healing process. If you decide that you do not need to apply a poultice then you may use a wound powder or gel such as Intrasite to apply to the wound and then dress or not as you wish. Most wounds do need to be kept covered whilst they heal purely because of the level of dirt and bacteria that is naturally contained in the field and stable environment. If you intend to apply a poultice then you should not treat the wound first with wound gel or any other antiseptic agent as the poultice contains its own chemicals.

Once you have cleaned a wound you can assess it better. Some wounds that appear trivial can actually turn out to be more serious whereas others that bleed profusely may not be. Depending on the severity of the injury, you may need to involve the vet for the following reasons:-

- The wound is deep enough to require stitching
- You think you will need antibiotics to treat any infection
- The wound has possibly affected some internal structures such as tendons or ligaments
- The wound is to the eye
- The bleeding is uncontrollable
- The injury involves a joint capsule or tendon sheath

Often a veterinary assessment of a wound is required to make sure that no further action is necessary. No-one wants to pay expensive vet bills – why do these things always happen over the weekend – but ultimately, it can cost you more in the long run to make a mistake when assessing a wound or injury and then embark upon a course of treatment that is not appropriate or insufficient. And of course the welfare of your Connemara pony should be your paramount concern.

Both uncontrollable bleeding and penetration of a joint or tendon sheath are classified as veterinary emergencies.

A small puncture wound to a joint will require hospitalization, as an injury of this nature can set up an infection in the closed joint capsule which cannot be controlled.

Clip the wound, clean it carefully and then cover it and prepare the horse for travel. The vet will need to flush the wound several times in a sterile, clinical environment and treat the horse with antibiotics. Hesitation and time loss in this situation can prove fatal, as the infection can ultimately become untreatable leading eventually to the loss of the horse. It is often the more insignificant injuries to joints that are the most serious and also by their nature, the easiest ones to miss.

Chapter 11: Minor Ailments

Bruises, knocks and bangs

Horses can very easily knock or bang their legs whilst playing in the field or perhaps striking into themselves when being ridden or jumping. A horse that becomes cast in the stable may also injure itself whilst trying to get up. Cast means that the horse is lying down and is unable to rise, usually because it is lying down in a corner of the stable and has gone to roll over and become trapped. Equally, a horse can also become trapped in the field environment, either caught up in fencing or in some kind of obstacle or natural hazard such as a pond or ditch.

A bang or bruise will usually manifest itself with heat and swelling. As with all equine injuries, it is important to make a careful assessment of the area to make sure that there is nothing more serious underlying. If the horse has had a knock, it may or may not be lame.

The treatment is much the same as for people which is:-

- Rest
- Cold treatment
- Compression

Clearly, you can't expect your horse to sit with its feet up but you can support the trauma with cold, compression and rest.

Rest can mean being confined to the stable or being turned out on limited pasture to restrict movement. Some horses are better turned out on a small area as they do not tolerate box rest, others will happily stay in the stable. Horses on box rest for a minor bruise or bang will benefit from walking in hand two or three times a day as this promotes the circulation and can help to bring down any swelling. Cold hosing clearly assists with this too and there are cold gels that you can apply topically to the horse's legs to help reduce heat and inflammation. Applying a light stable bandage overnight can help with support and also to reduce swelling and it is usual practice to put a stable bandage on the opposing leg as well, as the horse may be placing more weight on that in order to save the injured leg. Poorly applied bandages can cause more harm than good so it is important that you do not undertake this unless you are competent, otherwise you may end up causing issues such as pressure points over the tendons and ligaments which could prove to be more serious than the original injury that you are seeking to support.

Abscesses in the hoof
Every horse owner at some point in time has to deal with a hoof abscess. Abscesses are caused by some dirt or a foreign body working their way into the horse's hoof and thereby setting up an infection. Because the hoof is a closed capsule, the resultant build-up of pus and infection has nowhere to escape from and the horse as a consequence can become very lame. The lameness can be sudden onset and the horse may not want to weight bear. Lameness of this severity is often described as "fracture lame" hence the sense of rising panic in owners when their horse presents with this.

In fact, most abscesses are relatively easy to treat and usually a call to the farrier will cover it. The farrier will test your horse's hoof with a metal instrument called hoof testers and determine where the pain is emanating from and he can then pare away the foot until the infection is exposed, removing the shoe first if necessary. Pus will emerge, it may be darker or black in colour if it has been there a while and the relief to the horse will be immediate.

If your horse is shod and the farrier has had to remove the shoe, he may advocate leaving that foot shoe free until the infection has been dealt with, particularly if the abscess was under the shoe, as they can be. As with all wounds, it is important to assess that there is nothing more serious going on. For example, an abscess caused by a puncture wound which has in fact penetrated sensitive tissues deep within the hoof, would require prompt veterinary intervention and possibly X rays.

In the first instance, the area can be cleaned and flushed by hot tubbing the horse's foot. This is done by placing the affected hoof in a container of warm water with an additive such as Dettol or

Chapter 11: Minor Ailments

Savlon and encouraging the horse to stand a while with his hoof in the solution. The area should then be dried, dressed and poulticed in much the same way as you would clean and treat a wound on any other part of the horse's body. Because poultices applied to the sole of the hoof are difficult to keep in place and even harder to keep clean and dry, there are such things called Equiboots which can help. Equiboots are rigid hoof shaped boots which you can use to help contain a dressing or poultice, although if your horse will tolerate it, a nappy and a plastic bag can make an excellent practical alternative.

If the abscess has burst or been burst by the farrier, your horse should not require antibiotics. If an abscess is brewing then the vet may be reluctant to prescribe antibiotics which could impede the ripening effect of the abscess. It is usual and preferable to allow the abscess to mature and then burst and not interfere in this process by prescribing antibiotic medication.

Some abscesses seem to come from nowhere and you would have no idea one is brewing. In other situations, the horse may go on and off lame for a while before the abscess really starts to develop. It is usually said that there is heat to the hoof and a strong digital pulse in the horse's leg when an abscess is present, but this is not always the case. With some horses, there may be swelling or filling higher up the leg but this can vary from one horse to another.

The most common time of year for an abscess to form are the later winter months when the horses feet are generally just more waterlogged but this is not a hard and fast rule as a horse can develop an abscess at any time of year.

Respiratory issues

For such a large and robust animal, the horse has an amazingly sensitive and delicate system of airways which can easily become compromised by dust, mould spores, pollens and other environmental irritants.

Chapter 11: Minor Ailments

Horses have evolved to live permanently outside and so we compromise this by stabling them. We introduce a potentially restricted airflow and then offer them forage which may contain dust or mould such as poor quality hay. We can also ask them to perform athletic tasks, some of which may involve endurance and stamina.

All horses can at some point in their lives develop a cough. Sometimes this may be in response to a virus in much the same way as a human being can develop flu like symptoms such as nasal discharge and a cough. With support nursing and treatment, these issues should resolve in time. However it is also possible for a horse to develop a permanent cough, that can be likened to an asthma type response in humans to environmental conditions.

A horse's airway can become compromised by continued exposure to dust, mould spores, which can be found in hay and straw, and other pollutants. Some horses also show a response to pollens as they get older. This can result in inflammation to the upper or lower airways and then a cough will result. This condition is called Recurrent Airway Obstruction or RAO, it was formerly known as Chronic Obstructive Pulmonary Disorder or COPD, these are one in the same.

RAO in its early stages responds very well to management changes. The cough may only be occasional and if treated and managed early on, will not get worse. If RAO is left untreated whether through veterinary intervention or management changes, then it will worsen resulting in an animal with very limited exercise tolerance and a reduced quality of life. These animals will be described as "heaving" or having "heaves" and they will literally struggle for every breath. As the horse exhales or breathes out, there has to be a double effort to expel the air because of the narrowing and restriction of the airways hence the reference to heaving. Sometimes you can see a distinct line along the side of the horse's body as it exhales, this is called a heave line. The respiratory effort would be higher than that which should be seen in a mature resting horse which should be

Chapter 11: Minor Ailments

anywhere between eight to fifteen breaths per minute. A horse can only breath through its nose, it cannot breathe via the mouth.

A diagnosis of RAO can be made on clinical signs and/or by way of endoscopy, which is when a tube with a camera on the end of it is passed down through the horse's airways to the point where the trachea or windpipe reaches the lungs. The images presented are seen on a laptop in the clinic room and offer a first rate view of what is going on inside. This procedure can be performed under standing sedation. It is also possible during endoscopy to take what is called a tracheal wash, which is where a solution is flushed down through the endoscope and then sucked back up taking with it some of the cells which line the airways, these are then tested for their inflammatory properties and graded as to severity. A mild cough with some small presence of inflammatory cells may be treated in several ways:-

- Keeping the horse on grass rather than in the stable or increasing the time spent at grass if it is not possible for the horse to live out all the time
- Changing stable bedding to a dust extracted or dust free alternative, certainly avoid the use of straw
- Ensuring that the stable has adequate ventilation
- Try and ensure that the horse is not sharing any airspace with animals on other dusty bedding types as all your efforts will be in vain
- Feed soaked hay or haylage rather than dry hay. Hay needs to be soaked for a minimum of twenty minutes per day, preferably longer, and can be fed either on the floor in a container or loose or in a hay net
- Make sure all feeds are well dampened
- The vet may choose to support with medication, a favourite is Ventipulmin which has a human equivalent, and this is a broncho dilator and is designed to support the airway. Ventipulmin can also be combined with an antibiotic if there is a suspicion that infection is also present. Ventipulmin is a powder which may be added to the horse's feed

Chapter 11: Minor Ailments

- Adjust workloads accordingly. Horses with established RAO may not perform at the highest levels of athletic function but can happily work in different jobs where less is demanded of them
- Medication may also be dispensed more directly into the airways than across the digestive tract by the use of inhalers which are identical to the ones that are prescribed for asthma in people. These are dispensed to the horse via the nostril and by using something called a spacer device. The inhaler is placed in one end and the other end is placed over one of the horse's nostrils with a spare hand covering the horse's other nostril. Despite the evident restriction to the airway, most horses quickly learn to tolerate this procedure amazingly well
- For horses with a more advanced condition, there is a device which fits over the entire muzzle attached to the head by way of a leather strap behind the ears. This dispenses similar medication but by way of water vapour and this medium enables the drugs to penetrate further down the airways and into the horse's lungs

Managing a horse with an airway issue is perfectly possible and does not have to mean an end to the horse's working life. The key with this condition as in many others, is early intervention. Treatment means that any early damage is reversible and will not progress, failure to act ultimately causes degeneration and deterioration which will ultimately impact on the horse's quality of life and longevity.

Colic

Colic is one of the words that strikes fear into the heart of any horse owner, this is because it is potentially life threatening and can strike without warning even if your regime of care is competent and well informed.

Colic is a general term for abdominal pain and there are different types of colic:-

- Obstructive colic, in simple terms, a blockage. This can be caused by a mass of food, an internal issue such as a lipoma, which is a fatty lump common in older horses or a foreign object. It is also seen in older horses who are beginning to suffer from dental issues and who are therefore not chewing their food adequately as a consequence
- Gas colic, also known as spasmodic colic or tympanic colic. This is the build-up of gas within the horse's digestive tract which can be due to excessive fermentation or the inability to move the gas through effectively. It could be caused by an excessive time on pasture on spring grass, perhaps the administration of a tube of wormer which can affect some horses or the stress of travel or competition
- Sand colic. A build- up of sand or sandy earth caused by grazing pasture right down to soil level leading to the uptake of dirt and earth into the horse's system

Horses that are suffering from colic will exhibit a range of symptoms. In the early stages, the horse may seem a little disinterested in its surroundings, withdrawn, and not responding properly. If the colic progresses and the horse starts to suffer abdominal pain, the respiratory and heart rate will soon begin to rise, the horse will become unsettled and agitated and start to sweat and box walk. To try and relieve pain the horse may then begin rolling, getting up and then going down again repeatedly. If the pain levels become too great the horse may incur injuries in an attempt to relieve the pain.

Even a mild colic is a veterinary emergency because the situation can change from mild to serious very rapidly. Therefore, even if the horse is to be kept under observation, always phone your vet and alert them to the fact that you have a suspected colic and that a call out may be necessary. For a vet out in the field planning their calls, it can be helpful to know, as they can perhaps alter their visit list so they don't take that routine call on the other side

Chapter 11: Minor Ailments

of the county until later in the day so they are available for you if needed.

The key issue with a colic, apart from managing the situation quickly and effectively particularly in terms of the horse's pain, is to determine what type of colic it is as that dictates how the horse will be managed. For example with a gas or tympanic colic, support is usually given by the administration of a drug called Buscopan, which offers relief to the cramping and muscle spasm which can cause the horse so much pain. Most tympanic colics are treatable and the horse will recover fully unless there is another underlying cause.

Obstructive colics are more complicated, it is a question of trying to ascertain what the obstruction is and where it is. Partially chewed food matter can be helped on its way with the administration of liquid paraffin via a tube, this is called drenching. Surgery is also an option if drenching is unsuccessful. An obstruction caused by something like a lipoma, which is a harmless fatty mass, harmless that is until it causes a blockage in the horse's gut, may need surgical removal.

The decision to operate on a horse for colic is not one to be taken lightly but is one that needs to be taken quickly. An early diagnosis may give you the opportunity to travel a sick horse to hospital for surgery before the situation deteriorates beyond the point of no return. Survival rates following colic surgery are improving all the time but are dependent on factors other than the skill of the veterinary surgeons. The University of Liverpool, which has a pioneering veterinary hospital that regularly and successfully performs colic surgeries, lists these key factors as follows:-

- The type of colic
- The time since onset
- The horse's condition on admission

The type of things you as an owner will need to think about before embarking on colic surgery are:-

Chapter 11: Minor Ailments

- The age of the horse and any other pre-existing health conditions
- The recovery rate, bearing in mind the factors listed above
- Post-operative care and whether you can support the horse during this process which will last about 2-3 months
- The costs which will range anywhere from £3,000-£5,000 ($4706-$7843) and this will just be for the surgery. There will be hospital aftercare and monitoring and possibly follow up treatment as the horse recovers

Some owners feel with elderly or compromised horses – horses with other health issues – that it is not fair to put them through something with not a great chance of a good outcome. You have to outweigh the possible chances of a good outcome with the alternative, which is the stress caused to the horse by travelling it potentially some distance to hospital whilst it is suffering only to have to make that final decision. Sometimes it is better to simply intervene early and put them to sleep at home where they are in familiar surroundings and you can put an end quickly to any pain and suffering.

One of the reasons why owners fear colic so much is that sometimes it can appear for no apparent reason. Knowing the cause of the colic helps us to understand and potentially treat it but a colic that comes from nowhere is much more frightening. Some horses seem to be more prone to getting colic than others but the general principles of good horse management are the weapons of defence in your armoury to reduce the likelihood of a colic occurring, you can never remove the possibility of colic completely. Here are some golden rules to try and adhere to:-

- Introduce any change of feed gradually, over a period of 7-10 days
- ALWAYS ensure that the horse has access to long fibre at all times so feed hay ad lib including on the field when the grass is poor

- Learn to identify and then remove poisonous plants from your pasture
- Introduce a change of hay or haylage in a similar fashion to hard feed so over a course of days – even a bale of hay baled on a different part of the field on a different day can have a potentially distinct effect on the microbial population in the horse's hind gut
- Ensure that clean fresh water is available to the horse at all times
- Manage situations in a way that minimizes stress
- Ensure that the horse's teeth are checked regularly for its age and if you see the horse having any difficulty chewing then take action. A horse that has dental issues will try to chew and then drop food out of its mouth, this is termed "quidding". Or a horse that takes a little time to crunch a polo or a carrot might make one suspect that all is not quite right in his mouth
- Turn the horse out as much as possible. It is no coincidence that colic seems to be more prevalent in stable kept horses. Physical mobility promotes gut motility and it is the constant movement of the gut, entitled the peristaltic wave that keeps the food matter moving through
- Observation is key. If you know your horse, you will know if something is not quite right and this is a trigger to monitor the horse for any potential changes or developments. Early intervention is essential so always be on the alert for warning signs

Lameness

There are so many potential issues that can occur within the horse's foot and lower leg that they are too numerous to be covered within the pages of this book. However it is helpful to take an overview of some of the more common issues and how to manage them to best support a happy outcome.

Although 99% of lameness is generally within the foot, there are other issues which can occur higher up the horse's leg and you

Chapter 11: Minor Ailments

could do worse than study and learn the structure of the horse's leg below the knee and hock – the bones, tendons and ligaments with their points of origin and points of attachment. This will stand you in good stead later on.

The horse has no muscle below the knee and hock but he does have a structure of bones, tendons which are the "tails" of the muscles higher up the leg and ligaments. This narrow column of bones and soft tissues culminating in the hoof has to provide all of the support and power to the horse when it is static and in motion. There is amazing strength to this mechanism considering the forces that it has to bear when the horse is moving and turning at speed but also, there is vulnerability.

Lame horses are routinely referred to as "not sound" or "unsound", both terms mean the same thing. Lameness is usually graded out of a score of 10 so a horse will be described as being 1/10 lame or 4/10 lame or more depending on severity. The word "unlevel" also refers to lameness which is either more minor or more subtle – not the same thing necessarily at all and the phrase "bridle lame" refers to an irregularity in gait when the horse is under saddle, so being ridden. The horse may not actually be lame in this case at all, there may be a resistance causing this either in response to the rider or some other factor such as an ill-fitting saddle.

A horse can be lame in more than one leg at a time and can have different degrees of lameness in different legs for different reasons. If a horse is very lame then most owners can spot that, a more subtle lameness is much harder to detect and may not be easily apparent, only visible to a trained eye. The main issue to consider when a horse is lame is the cause as this will determine what you do next, principally can you continue to turn your horse out or should he be restricted to the stable.

A lame horse might be lame with something that is quite minor such as:-

Chapter 11: Minor Ailments

- A bruise on the sole caused by treading on a stone or being ridden generally over rough ground
- A corn which is a bruise or trauma to the seat of corn which is an area on the sole of the horse' hoof so called on either side of the horse's frog up near the heel. Corns do take longer to resolve
- An overreach. This is where the horse catches or strikes the back of one of the front hooves with a hind hoof and causes bruising or an actual wound on the heel area of the front hoof
- Soreness after shoeing, some horses can be quite "footy" after shoeing and shorten their stride for a few days
- Mud rash or mud fever. This is caused by continuous exposure to wet conditions which makes the skin on the horse's lower leg soften, allowing the bacteria Dermatophilus congolensis to penetrate via small scratches or abrasions. This will result in a bacterial infection which causes soreness, itching and scabs. If left untreated, mud fever can become quite an unpleasant issue for the horse resulting in odema and inflammation, often requiring the intervention of a vet. It is not generally a serious condition but can require quite a lot of time and effort to resolve
- Thrush. A bacterial sometimes fungal infection of the soft area on the sole of the horse's hoof so in and around the region called the frog

In addition to minor conditions, there are a range of more serious issues resulting from injury or wear and tear:-

- Sprains or strains to tendons and ligaments contained within the lower leg; anything from a minor "tweak" to a complete breakdown of the tendon or ligament
- Inflammatory or degenerative conditions affecting the soft tissue structures
- Fracture to one of the bones below the knee or hock. There is a long bone called the cannon bone which connects the knee or hock to the fetlock joint then beneath

the fetlock, there is the long pastern bone, the small pastern bone and the pedal bone within the hoof. There is also a small bone called the navicular bone which sits behind the joint between the short pastern and the pedal bone
- Degenerative conditions of any of the bones within the limb or the joints between them, these conditions may involve the surrounding soft tissue supports as well. Some examples of these would be navicular syndrome, pedalostitis, ringbone and sidebone

These lists are not exhaustive nor are they intended to be, they are simply designed to provide you with some examples of what might be a major or a minor condition so you can see the distinction.

What should you do if your Connemara pony is lame?
The first thing to do is to observe your horse and see if you can establish which leg the horse is lame on. Pick up the foot and examine it. The lameness could be caused by something as simple as a stone lodged in the hoof.

If the lameness is clearly evident so that you can identify the leg in question then once you have examined the foot, have a good look round the limb for any evidence of trauma or injury, any heat or swelling and any response to pain. See if there is an evident digital pulse in the lame leg; the digital pulse may be felt just behind the fetlock, a slight or light pulse is normal so it is good practice to learn what is normal for your pony so that you can assess any difference.

If you are not sure which leg the pony is lame on then a "trot up" might reveal more and this is something your vet will certainly do if you have recourse to them.

Trotting a horse up
Trot up is when a horse is assessed for soundness. This may be because it is suspected that the horse is lame or because the horse is part way through a competition such as eventing or endurance

Chapter 11: Minor Ailments

riding and the rules state that the horse must be demonstrably sound before it is allowed to progress to the next stage of the competition.

A trot up does not have to be performed in front of a vet. A competent and experienced owner may ask a colleague or friend to trot their horse up on the yard because it doesn't feel quite right. It can take time to develop an eye for soundness but it is quite fascinating looking at lots of different horses and assessing how they move.

In order to trot a horse up successfully, you should have access to a hard and level concrete area similar to a road way. The area must be safe as you could be trotting up a horse that has been on box rest for several weeks and trotting may be the last thing on his mind once he is liberated from his stable! For that reason, it is usual to trot the horse up in a bridle so there is maximum control and for the safety of the handler, it is advisable to wear a hat and gloves.

Most good veterinary practices have a dedicated lameness assessment area. This will include what is called a concrete runway where the horse can be trotted up, and often this has a very minimal incline on it, a concrete square at one end where the horse can be lunged on a circle on the hard and an arena or artificial surface at the other end where the horse can be assessed on soft level ground. Different surfaces give different information about the potential cause of lameness and this procedure is always undertaken first before recourse to other diagnostic techniques such as nerve blocking, x rays and MRI scans.

For an owner presented with a lame horse at home, there could be an absolute myriad of causes and unless it is something clearly evident then you will probably need to take further advice. An example of a clearly evident minor issue would be an overreach when the horse has come back from work or come in from the field. An obvious cause of a serious injury would be a swelling to the soft tissues behind the cannon bone, indicating damage to the tendons or ligaments. In the first scenario, you will be able to treat

Chapter 11: Minor Ailments

the wound and return the horse to the stable or the field. In the second situation, the horse must be immediately immobilized and restricted to prevent further damage from occurring and veterinary advice sought.

If you are presented with a lame horse and you cannot obviously ascertain the cause of the lameness then it is advisable to confine the horse to the stable pending further investigation; if the cause of the issue is something trivial then it will not do the horse any harm to be stabled. If it is serious then you will certainly have prevented a bad situation from getting worse.

It is essential to try and get a diagnosis of the problem as soon as you can otherwise any action or treatment that you implement or don't implement may prove harmful. Sometimes it is a question of waiting to see what happens or develops – don't expect your vet to have second sight, they can't see inside the foot. Time is often the best way to reveal the problem and your vet can advise you what you should do with the horse in the meantime. Options may be:-

- Total box rest
- Box rest with limited walking in hand two or three times a day
- Restricted turnout so turning out onto a small and confined area in circumstances that will not encourage uncontrolled exercise so may be with a favourite companion
- Return to the field

Your vet may recommend support, perhaps by cold hosing or stable bandaging and also the inclusion of Phenylbutazone in the horse's feed. Phenylbutazone or "bute" is a non-steroidal anti-inflammatory drug. It is quite a slow acting anti-inflammatory but does also offer good pain relief. The use of bute is debatable as if the horse needs to be taken into hospital for further assessment then it is preferable that bute is absent from his system so that the lameness work up can be fully assessed without any pain relieving medication which might influence the diagnosis. Bute will not mask anything serious such as a blown tendon or a fractured bone so do not fear that you will disguise something major.

Often if a vet is unsure what the cause is, he will take the standard line of bute and 7 days box rest followed by re-assessment. It is frustrating and often worrying when you have a lame horse without diagnosis but diagnosis must be logical and coherent otherwise it is of no value and so it is fairly standard to follow this protocol in the absence of something that is very evident to detect.

Referral to hospital
A lameness that is unresponsive to treatment or cannot be diagnosed at home will ultimately result in a referral to an equine veterinary hospital. This may or may not be your own practice; your vet might seek to refer you to a particular location or specialist vet depending on the issues that he suspects.

Irrespective of what has gone beforehand, the referring vet or even your own vet within the hospital environment will begin the assessment by trotting the horse up again. Lameness investigations or work ups as they can be called, will usually involve the vet and a veterinary nurse who will handle the horse for you, this allows the owner to remain with the vet so that they can discuss what they find as the investigation progresses. The trot ups usually follow a set pattern:-

- Examination of the horse at rest, palpating (feeling) limbs and assessing the horse's conformation which means the way the horse is put together; conformation can have a bearing on soundness issues. The vet will be looking for any heat or swelling, he may assess the digital pulse which can be felt behind the fetlock and he may also use hoof testers. If the horse is shod then the vet may remove the shoe on the affected hoof but he might wait first to see the horse trotted up before doing this, as taking the shoe away can have a bearing on how the horse then moves
- Walking the horse away and walking the horse back in a straight line, this may be done several times at the request

Chapter 11: Minor Ailments

of the vet. When the horse is turned at the end of the run, it is always turned away from the handler and this also gives the vet an opportunity to see the horse load bearing on the turn which provides more information
- Once the horse has been seen in walk, the vet will ask the handler to repeat the process in trot, again the horse may be trotted back and forth several times.
- There is also the option to lunge the horse in a small circle on a concrete surface and similarly on a soft surface.

The trot up is the initial assessment, which is designed to provide clues as to where to look next; sometimes it provides sufficient information but not always.

Following the trot up, the vet has other diagnostic options available to him:-

- Nerve blocks
- X Rays
- MRI scanning

Nerve Blocks
This is the injection of a routine anaesthetic agent into part of the horse's limb which will temporarily remove pain from the affected area. The injection will work within a few minutes and then the horse is trotted up again. The vet usually starts in the foot, as most lameness problems occur there unless there are compelling reasons to suspect an issue at a point higher up the leg. If the horse goes sound on the trot up then the correct area or joint on the horse's leg has been identified as the culprit. The vet is able to inject and numb different structures within the foot itself to help diagnosis. Nerve blocks in themselves are only a diagnostic tool which help the vet pinpoint the area he think needs further investigation, they will only direct you to an area of concern, they are not a diagnosis in their own right.

X Rays
Radiography will only allow the vet to look at the bones in the foot and the lower limb and nothing further. He can look at the

Chapter 11: Minor Ailments

joints between the bones and also the surface of the bones for information. X rays can be taken from several different angles to aid diagnosis.

MRI scanning

The advent of MRI scanning in horse's hooves revolutionized lameness investigation and hooves are probably the most common part of the horse's body that is routinely scanned. But again as with nerve blocking and X rays, MRI scanning is only a diagnostic tool and the interpretation of the results is key. An MRI scan may show several "hot spots" in the hoof, it is determining which one is relevant that is critical.

Referring a horse to hospital for an undiagnosed lameness can be a very worrying and expensive time for any owner. Not knowing what may be wrong is sometimes worse than hearing bad news. Any diagnosis must be put into the context of what the horse can usefully do; many older horses would show up as at least unlevel if you trotted them on a concrete surface, an MRI scan may show several hot spots and X rays would be bound to reveal some bony changes within the foot, it does not mean that the horse cannot continue to have a useful and happy life with a level of work appropriate to its issues, supported with the correct care and veterinary input. As with conditions in people, management is the key to the horse's welfare and longevity.

Fly/insect predation

Horses can be completely plagued by a variety of flies during the warmer months and some horses suffer quite badly from fly bites and associated skin reactions. Reactions can vary from small bites to large hives, which may require treatment with antihistamines. Different flies seem to trouble different horses differently! Some horse flies seem to love bay horses which can react quite badly to their bites whereas other horses of a different colour in the same field are far less troubled by them.

Fly bites can cause a number of issues for the owner to manage ranging from general discomfort and itchiness in the horse to

Chapter 11: Minor Ailments

actual infection. Some horses can become so distressed by the presence of flies that they will actually end up injuring themselves in order to get away from them.

As with any health issue, prevention is always better than cure. There are many different types of fly rug available on the market which can provide differing levels of protection to the horse. Don't forget to include your Connmera pony's face and eyes – some horses suffer terribly from fly predation around their eyes and you can fit a mask to protect them.

Fly spray is another option although it is generally considered amongst the horse owing community that most sprays do not work and they cost a lot of money as well. A tour around social media sites will find you some recipes for homemade fly spray, worth trying and seeing which ones seem to be effective. Beware using strong chemicals such as Deet which is contained in a number of branded fly sprays, this can cause skin reactions and irritations to some horses.

In particularly hot and fly blown weather, bring your pony in to offer respite from the conditions. In hot weather, horses need shade and respite from both the sun and the flies so if your pony is in at night and out in the day, consider swapping that round so that you turn him out at nightfall and bring back in at first light to spend the day in the stable.

Chapter 12: Saying Goodbye

It is an inevitable part of horse ownership that we have to say goodbye to our beloved animals when the times comes. As a horse owner, it is always worth being prepared for this, as death can come suddenly and being caught without any foresight or planning can make a very stressful situation, ten times worse. It is particularly important as a first time owner that you spend a little time thinking over the alternatives for your pony and making yourself aware of who you would call and where you can find the right information and having gone through that exercise, forget about it until you need to remember.

There are several different terms which refer to the cessation of life – putting to sleep, putting down, humane destruction, euthanasia – they all mean the same thing. There are also different methods of putting a horse down and the one that is chosen will depend partly on circumstances and partly on your own preference.

The majority of horses do not die naturally, they either succumb to disease or injury and it would be inhumane to allow life to continue or they simply become too old to have a viable quality of life. However the phrase "a viable quality of life" does not just apply to elderly horses, it can be applied to an equine of any age whose ability to enjoy life as a horse is compromised for some reason. Sometimes these are the hardest decisions to make as it seems almost unfair to put down a young horse but there may be compelling reasons to do so such as a disease or illness that cannot be successfully treated or a serious injury.

There are two ways to put a horse to sleep:-

- Lethal injection
- Humane killer (gun)

Chapter 12: Saying Goodbye

Lethal Injection

A horse can be put to sleep via lethal injection and this may only be administered by a vet.

The injection works by administering a lethal overdose of anaesthetic agents to the horse, which induces rapid unconsciousness followed by cardiovascular arrest. If the horse is not already recumbent, he will go down pretty quickly and life will cease rapidly, usually within minutes. The injection is given intravenously into a vein, although sometimes a catheter is used. On occasion, the unconscious horse will need a second dose of the lethal agent in order to stop the heart. If the horse is a little anxious about what is happening then he may be sedated first.

Humane killer or gun

The other option is to shoot the horse using a specially modified gun also called a humane killer, your vet can put a horse to sleep via either of these methods but there are other people who can shoot the horse, they are called knackermen or slaughtermen– they are usually very efficient at it as they do it regularly, they will also be putting down fallen stock such as farm animals. You need to hold a valid firearms licence in order to be allowed to end life via this method. However, a firearms licence on its own is not sufficient competency to perform this task.

If your horse is put down by a bullet to the head then a vet may wish to administer a little sedation first, as it is important that the horse keeps his head very still. The muzzle of the gun is placed directly onto the horse's forehead and a bullet is discharged straight into the horse's brain, death is instantaneous. There may be some bleeding from the bullet hole and the nostrils, which can vary from a trickle to quite a lot.

Whichever method you choose is really down to you unless the circumstances dictate that one of those methods is not an option but the welfare of your pony must always take priority over human preferences. Shooting sounds violent and it is a violent act on one level but it is also completely instant and many people

Chapter 12: Saying Goodbye

prefer it for that reason to the option of lethal injection. Without advocating voyeurism, it is helpful to perhaps see someone else's horse put down before you have to face it with your own, this will help prepare you and you will know what to expect. You will be more detached as it is not your horse. Discuss options with your vet ahead of time and as part of gathering information; that will help you to make an informed decision about which method you prefer if you are able to make a choice when the time comes.

Sometimes these events occur suddenly, so for example a colic or a broken leg, sometimes they have to be planned because a horse is just simply too old or too arthritic to carry on happily. In either scenario, it is not an easy thing to do but you have to view it as the last gift you give to your horse – better to be a day too early than a month too late.

Wherever you choose to euthanase the horse, you should try and ensure that it is within a soft area where there is room for all parties concerned to be present in safety. You may also need to choose a location that has good vehicular access depending on what you plan to do with the horse's body afterwards. The vet has a duty to ask you what your plans are for disposal afterwards as it is part of his remit to ensure that appropriate arrangements have been made before he puts the horse down.

You need to consider very carefully whether you want to be present when the horse is put down or whether actually you will cause distress to the horse by becoming emotional – remember the horse does not know what is happening. Many owners will remain present but then absent themselves when the horse has passed away and the body is removed. You can plan to have a friend with you for support but if you get caught up in a crisis, it may be that that friend cannot be with you so you need to consider the situation all ways round.

With either option, you may hold the horse but the vet will ask you to stand well back as the horse goes down purely because it is not always certain which way they will fall if they are being put down by lethal injection. Most buckle their knees as if they were

Chapter 12: Saying Goodbye

going down in the stable to roll and then go over onto their sides but others can go back onto their haunches and then go over sideways so human safety is paramount.

If the horse has been injected, he will continue to take a few deep breaths, which will become slower and then cease. There will be a final expiration a few minutes after the horse has passed away and also air turbulence at the nostrils, which is simply the residual air leaving the lungs, it is not really a breath as such but it can surprise people if they are not aware the horse will do this. The vet will check the horse's heartbeat with a stethoscope and confirm that the horse has passed away. The vet will remain with the horse until all external movement has ceased. Minor muscle tremors and twitching of the nostrils can occur for a short time after death, these are reflex actions and do not indicate that the euthanasia has been unsuccessful.

Horses that have been together for a long time will grieve when one of their group has gone and so it is best to let them see the horse when it has passed away because it can help them understand why that horse is no longer there. Allowing them into the field to have a sniff and an inspection is a good plan, just letting them have some time with their old friend. If the horse has a long standing companion and is to be put down by lethal injection then it may be appropriate to allow the companion to be present at a safe distance when euthanasia takes place. Thought must be given to finding a new companion for a horse that is left alone, preferably prior to the event if it is planned as this makes the loss even harder. Donkeys form very strong emotional attachments to other donkeys and horses and are said to grieve more deeply than horses. Some horses will go off their food for a few days even if they have other established company.

There are really three main options of disposing of the horse's body once it has been put down and once again this decision is usually governed by practicality and to some extent, the owner's preference.

- Burial

- Cremation
- Incineration

Burial

You will usually only be able to bury your horse if the horse passes away on your own property and is classified as a pet. A privately owned horse is classified as a pet but a riding school horse used in the course of a business for example is not.

If you want to bury your horse you need to be prepared and have a friendly digger driver available, preferably at short notice. It is best to warn him in advance about what he is going to be doing. There is no two ways about it, the removal of a horse to a freshly dug grave is not a nice process and most owners, even if they have been present when the horse is put down, choose to absent themselves at this point.

Having dug a suitably sized pit and hopefully avoided any pipe work of significance, the horse is moved by attaching "strops" around its body with someone holding the horse's head; a strop is a broad webbing line with a metal clasp at the end so it can be adjusted to different sizes. The horse can be lifted by suspending it on the bucket of the digger and then lowered gently into the grave. The digger driver will then cover the horse by replacing the excavated earth.

You may not be able to bury your pony if you are adjacent to a waterway or river, even if it is your own land. The National Rivers Authority in the UK can provide more information on this. And for more general advice, speak to DEFRA in the UK, the Department for the Environment, Farming and Rural affairs.

Cremation

There are many licensed pet crematoria that have facilities for dealing with large animals and they will come and collect the horse for you after it has been put down. Some of them are able to euthanase the horse as well first but this would not be via lethal injection as only a vet can do this.

Chapter 12: Saying Goodbye

The horse is removed into the back of a specially adapted vehicle in the same way that they remove fallen livestock, which is by attaching a chain around its body and winching it on. Again this is a time when most owners choose not to be present as it is not a pleasant process.

You can elect to have your horse cremated individually or with others, the cost can reach several hundred pounds if you opt to have the horse cremated on its own and if your horse dies suddenly and without warning, individual cremation may not be possible. A box of ashes will be returned to you, don't be surprised at how large it is. Most pet crematoria give you the option of different types of box and an engraved brass plaque as well and some will cut a section of the horse's tail and return it tied with a piece of ribbon.

Disposal by the knackerman

The knackerman is the name of the man who disposes of fallen stock, usually farm animals. Don't write them off in preference to the vet as they are very experienced at their job. They are not able to put the horse down by injection, only a vet can do that. Most carcasses that the knackerman disposes of will be incinerated or rendered. Horses that have been put down by lethal injection must be incinerated if collected by the knackerman due to the presence in the horse's system of the chemical agents. This is one of the cheapest options for disposal with private cremation being usually the most expensive.

What happens if my pony dies in hospital?

In this situation, you will be unlikely to be able to opt for burial at home because of the practical logistics of removal of the body, so usually the choices would be limited to cremation or removal by the knackerman. Your veterinary practice will be very experienced at managing this situation as they will have done it many times before and they will be able to guide you through the practicalities if your pony dies in hospital.

Insurance Claims

Whether or not your costs will be covered depends upon the circumstances of your pony's death and the type of policy that you hold.

All insurance companies will need to be told that your pony is no longer alive, as the cover will cease and the policy will need to be terminated.

Whether or not you can claim for your costs will depend upon the type of cover you hold and whether or not you have obtained the insurer's agreement prior to the pony being put down. If you are not sure, talk to your insurers beforehand so you understand the implications of what you are doing or the circumstances in which payment will be made in the event of the death. It is easier to have these conversations in the cold light of day when the pony is happily grazing in the field than when the event is imminent and you are upset. Take notes when you talk to the insurer and file them away with the policy so that you can refer to them months or years down the line. Check at renewal that the cover has not changed at all and that your understanding of the policy terms and conditions is still clear, as your insurance cover may vary from year to year based on if nothing else, the age of the pony.

The insurance company will require a veterinary certificate before they will consider making a payment for value and/or costs. In some situations, they may also require a post mortem to be carried out, usually if the cause of death is not known or is in doubt.

Counselling and support

For some people, the loss of their horse is truly overwhelming and they need more professional support than that which can be offered by friends and family. Your vet may be able to put you in touch with an appropriate organization or individual who can offer support to you through this difficult time. An Internet search will reveal that there are many counsellors offering support to those who have lost an animal so you are not alone.

Chapter 12: Saying Goodbye

For many of us our horses, as with other animals, are part of our family. And as horses take up such an enormous amount of time in terms of their care, the loss of a horse can leave a huge void in the owner's life which only serves to emphasise the loss.

And perhaps having to put a horse to sleep is made worse because of their sheer size and the practical difficulties that attach to the task, particularly if the horse's death has been unexpected and therefore not at a time or in a location of the owner's choosing.

Horses enjoy a different quality of life and lifestyle to a cat or a dog and so what may be an acceptable decision for a companion animal whose lifestyle is perhaps more sedentary, is not necessarily the right option for a horse. But with any animal, it is important to remember that they don't reflect on their mortality but simply want a good life rather than necessarily a long life and to be free of pain – ending an unacceptable quality of life or removing pain from illness or injury is the last gift you can give your horse.

The British Horse Society in the UK has developed a scheme called "Friends at the End". There are more than 100 volunteer welfare officers who have undergone training and who are located all over the UK who not only can be with you when the time comes but can also discuss the options with you prior to euthanasia. Although it is advisable to give the matter at least a small amount of thought, many people do not and put off facing that awful day and as a consequence can be unprepared which only makes it worse.

"Friends at the End" will support horse owners through that difficult process of saying goodbye. Some people may be unable to keep their horse for other reasons such as ill health or financial reasons and Friends at the End will talk through other options that may be appropriate in those circumstances.

If the horse does need to be put down then many Friends can be available on the day to help support the owner and will even hold the horse if the owner does not feel able to. For many people, it is a comfort to know that the horse is with another horse lover and experienced equine person.

Senior Executive (BHS Welfare) Lee Hackett said: "All of our Friends at the End have lost horses themselves and received training from bereavement counsellors so they really do understand the feelings of loss and grief that come when a horse dies. They aren't there to take the place of a counsellor or vet, but they can offer an extra source of support. At the hardest time in a horse owner's journey our Friends are available to make it as smooth and straightforward as possible."

Keepsakes

There are a number of keepsakes available which can be made from the tail hair from your pony, some people just cut a section to keep but you can get this transformed into a unique and special item of jewellery.

There are a number of companies that offer a range of distinctive items, they tightly braid and twist the hair into different shapes to form necklaces, bracelets and rings to which charms or other details can be added. For many people, this is a touching way to remember their horse, particularly because jewellery is such a personal item worn next to the skin.

This is not the only way to honour and remember a lost animal. Some people plant a tree or, if the horse is buried at home, mark the spot with a stone slab.

And some owners choose to remember their beloved horse by offering a cup or trophy at a local show that the horse was particularly associated with or a class at a certain show that their horse had a connection to.

Chapter 13: Costs

Costs can be divided into five main categories:-

- Initial outlay
- One off start-up costs
- Known regular costs
- Indeterminate regular costs
- Unforeseen bills

Initial outlay

Your main initial outlay is going to be the purchase of your Connemara pony and this can range in price from a few hundred pounds or dollars to several thousand. You will also need to allocate funds for the cost of the pre-purchase vetting or vettings if you have more than one and a vetting will cost you in the region of £150-£300 ($235-$470), as already discussed.

One off start-up costs

This will include your saddlery and any other equipment such as grooming kits, rugs and yard items. If you are starting from scratch, a really comprehensive wish list could hit your wallet for as much as £2,000 ($3154) - a new saddle alone can cost in the region of £1,000 ($1577) or more but the idea is that once these items have been purchased, with care, you should not need to replace them for a very long time. It is not necessary to buy everything new either and careful shopping can mean these costs can be reduced as much as possible.

Known regular costs

This will include things like your insurance if you are paying monthly, your farrier and your feed/hay bills. Sometimes it is easier to budget by arranging these costs where possible on a

Chapter 13: Costs

monthly basis so a monthly Direct Debit for your insurance premium and a monthly delivery of hay and feed. Some people who do not want to insure their horses will make a monthly payment to their veterinary practice as a type of advance payment against future veterinary costs or simply pay a monthly sum into a savings account so that there is a nest egg ready for unexpected bills.

It is tricky to put precise figures on monthly costs as there is so much variation. For instance, how much hay you feed will depend on the season, the prevailing weather, how much work your horse is doing and the price of hay which varies year to year according to supply, type and location. One can find similar variants when looking at insurance premiums and vets bills too. However I think it would be safe to say that a monthly figure of £250 ($378.45) is an appropriate average to act as a guide for the first time horse owner.

Indeterminate regular costs

These will include things like bedding, although many people budget on a monthly/weekly basis and rigidly stick to their allocation. Hay and to some extent feed can also be a moveable feast in terms of cost as the amount of hay fed can depend on the weather and the time of year.

Unforeseen bills

Usually these will relate to vets bills and uninsured bills can be very large so it is sensible to have some sort of contingency fund or spare credit card for a rainy day. If you do get saddled with a large and unexpected vet's bill, most practices understand enough to allow owners to make an arrangement with them to pay by installments.

Budgeting

It is sensible to set some budget targets as horses are expensive to keep and it is easy for costs to spiral out of control. There are many ways to save money and reduce costs:-

Chapter 13: Costs

- Saving money around the yard
- Yard Equipment
- The Muck Heap
- Going Green
- Worming
- Tack and Equipment
- First Aid
- Bedding
- Feeding
- Your community

Saving money around the yard

Livery costs will be one of your largest expenses but there are ways to reduce these.

- Consider moving your horse to a cheaper yard. Be brutally honest with yourself, do you really need all these facilities. If you are a leisure rider that only rides at the weekend, why are you paying for an indoor school, two outdoor schools and a cross country course
- Consider switching your horse from full livery to part or assisted livery and doing some of the work yourself. Buddy up with a friend on the yard to share the burden and split it between you
- Take the plunge and go DIY, this is immensely rewarding, not just because of the money you will save but also the time you will spend with your horse
- If you have some time, offer to work part-time on the yard in order to off-set some of your livery costs
- If the yard is part of a riding school then you could put your horse on working livery which will cut the costs even more. This is particularly helpful in the winter months when it is much harder to find the time to ride, it means your horse is being exercised and your livery bill is reducing
- Jump ship and go down on the farm. Probably less facilities but I expect the hacking is fabulous, you will

have access to hay and straw and probably unlimited turnout, from your horse's perspective, this is what he would choose
- If you are fortunate enough to keep your horses at home, then consider renting out some grazing and/or a stable to bring in extra income. You may find that the benefit of this is not just financial as having another pair of hands around to cover the yard when you can't, can be very beneficial

Yard Equipment

Yard equipment is expensive but essential and it also works hard on a daily basis, so when it breaks, what are the alternatives to going out and making an expensive purchase?

Yard sales are a good source of used equipment such as wheelbarrows and tools. Some local auction rooms will sell outdoor equipment as part of their general household sales and these auctions are also a good route to find more heavyweight items such as muck trailers and electrical/petrol driven equipment. Farm sales, usually held down on the farm, can sometimes include equine items so it is always worth keeping an eye out in the local press for these, you might find some random equine lots included amongst the agricultural items.

Social media is a great way to connect to other local equestrian people. There are thousands of horsey groups on Facebook and as well as advice and information, they are also a great place to buy and sell items in your locality. Yard equipment plus saddlery and everything else connected with horses.

The website Freecycle is even better as all items are free to the collector so keep a watch on your local groups and snap things up as they become available. If you see a bargain then grab it, even if you don't need it now, you may well do in the future as a replacement for a broken item and you have nothing to lose because it's free. There may be several Freecycle groups in your geographical area so see if you can become a moderator of one or more of them, this means that you approve the posts as they arrive, it is not a time consuming task. You will then be really well placed to spot any bargains even before the post has gone live.

The Muck Heap

If you have to pay to have your muck heap removed then consider trying to do a deal with your local farmer; often if you can cart it to the farm, then an arable farmer will take it particularly if they have no livestock of their own and therefore no ready access to manure. There are some farmers who will take it away for free but they are a rare breed!

Local gardening clubs and horticultural societies can often be interested in muck on a help yourself basis, it doesn't have to be straw based either. Put a notice in your local shop or Post Office or in the village magazine if you have one or contact local organisations via social media, you can even put it on Freecycle if you are not charging for it. It might not seem much of a dent in a big pile but it can make an impact if you have people coming in regularly and remember, it is less that you have to pay to have carted away. You can always bag it up and sell it or give it away to passing traffic at the garden gate.

Going Green

If you have your horses at home and have several, it might be worth investigating the use of muck or manure as fuel for a biomass boiler to heat your house. Clearly there may be hefty initial start-up costs but there are government grants and incentives available in the UK to encourage people to look at alternative ways to heat their home. Mucking out straight from the yard into the boiler as it were might give a whole new appeal to such a tedious task! Why stop there? What about solar panels on the stable roof? You might not want them on your house but you can put them on the stables. And perhaps even a mini wind turbine in the paddock. Making use of your land in this way is a sensible and a very environmentally friendly way to help offset some of your bills.

Worming

If you keep your horses on land that you own or rent or you are allocated your own grazing on a livery yard, you may find it cheaper to simply worm count your Connemara pony rather than worm every 6-8 weeks.

My horses have not had a routine commercial wormer in 8 years!! They are wormed for tapeworm spring and autumn as tapeworm does not show up on an FEC (Faecal egg count) and encysted red worm in December again, because that can evade detection on a worm count too. If your Connemara pony's worm count is low then you do not need to worm. It's easy, the lab will send you a kit and you return to them a small sample of droppings and they test it for you. I worm count mine every 4 months, used to be every 3 but they are a settled population with no visiting horses that graze and the droppings are removed from the fields regularly.

A worm count will cost you around the same as a tube of wormer but you will pay this cost much less frequently and the horses avoid the need to ingest all those unnecessary chemicals. I have never had a result that is higher than less than 50 epg (eggs per gram). There is now a new test for tapeworm the presence of which is detected by analysing a sample of the horse's saliva but this is still more expensive than actually buying a tube of tapeworm treatment.

Tack and Equipment

- Plan ahead and try and buy replacement rugs at the end of the season when old stock is being sold off at a discounted rate
- Mend and repair rugs whenever you can, we like shiny new rugs but your Connemara pony doesn't care what he wears as long as it is warm and comfortable
- Have a really good clear out once a year, it is amazing what you will find lurking in your tack room that you don't actually use. Be brave and head to a horsey car boot with all your surplus items and make sure you don't come

Chapter 13: Costs

back with more purchases unless they are absolutely necessary
- Sources items in the flesh at local saddleries and shows and then when you know what the correct sizing is, look on line to see if you can buy the same product more cheaply but beware postage and packing costs. A popular website for good value is www.equestrianclearance.com
- If you do buy online, then try and shop with other friends as sometimes the delivery charges are at a flat rate so the more you buy the greater the spread of the postage costs and with some companies, if you go over a certain value, then you can qualify for free delivery
- Sometimes local horse auctions will also have a section for saddlery, a great place for buying and selling
- Look on sites like eBay and Preloved for job lots of equestrian items for sale, usually someone that has had a tack room clear out and just can't be bothered or doesn't have the time to list all the items for sale separately. Sort, clean and then sell individually keeping anything that you might need yourself. Keep an alert on the site for anything that comes up on "local pick up" as this means you can go and look at it before purchase and you will also save delivery charges
- Try and layer rugs rather than purchase expensive rugs of different weights. We all know how much the temperature can fluctuate on the yard over the course of a day and how much easier we find it to just be able to shed layers or add them. Well it's the same for the horse and more efficient and quicker for the groom as well to quickly add or remove a rug. Use old, thin rugs as liners
- Clean and proof your own rugs rather than sending them away at the end of the season. Its hard work but your elbow grease is free. Use a car hose and a livestock shampoo and then re-proof when dry in the long summer months
- If you are on a big yard, see if you can get enough people together to buy a second hand industrial washer, this

would at least cover the bulk of your stable rugs and you can also use it for saddle cloths and numnahs
- With the best will in the world, items can wander off on livery yards so mark all of your equipment clearly so there is no doubt who it belongs to

First Aid

If you read the pharmaceutical company catalogues, they would have you believe that you need a veterinary box the size of a war chest in order to care for your Connemara pony. In fact, many of these items are just nice additional extras but you can do without them. However, there are staple things that no vet box should be without, the challenge is working out what you definitely need and what is just an expensive luxury item and what are the clever tricks that experienced yard owners use to keep their costs down.

Sometimes it is possible to substitute cheaper items for the ones that you are using or "human" items which are the same or similar to "equine" ones – remember if it says horse on it, it is bound to be double the price!

Here are some tips to save money.

- If you need to keep a hoof covered and dry after an abscess, a nappy is an excellent all in one dressing and protection to do this and it is flexible to fit around the horse's hoof, top it off with a supermarket plastic bag if your horse will tolerate it
- After changing a wound dressing in the morning prior to turnout, use vet wrap to keep the new dressing secure and in place whilst the horse is in the field. In the evening when the dressing is changed again and the horse is stabled overnight, dispense with the expensive vet wrap and use fibregee and a stable bandage whilst the horse is in the box – cheap, washable and re-usable, all the things that vet wrap is not, the moral is only vet wrap when you cannot put on a stable bandage i.e. during turnout.

Chapter 13: Costs

- Have a look in chemists for any articles that you use that have human usage as well, it is much cheaper to buy from a chemist than a saddler or an online equine store.
- If your pony is on regular medication, ask your vet for a written prescription which you can then use at an online pharmacy. You will have to pay a fee for the written prescription but they usually have several repeats on them and the savings you may make by buying the drugs elsewhere will easily outweigh the cost of the prescription. Remember though that your vet does need to see the pony every six months as a pre-requisite to prescribing so don't get caught out, if your prescription is running out and your pony has not needed to see the vet for a few months then they will not renew it without a visit out to see your horse. Don't forget to factor in postage to your costs as well
- If your pony requires an item after a trip to the vet, ask them whether they can help you source a cheaper alternative. As an example, a horse that is prescribed human asthma medication via an inhaler device will need a spacer to dispense the medication via the nostril. Equi-inhalers cost about £100 but you can buy a device for an infant that is unable to form a seal with their mouth and which does the job just as well placed over one of the horses' nostrils from your local chemist for under £10
- There are loads of different types of sterile pre-packaged wound dressings. One or two in a First Aid box is sensible but if your horse has a wound which requires the dressing changed once or twice daily then this can become very expensive. One of the best ways around this is a nice large roll of veterinary gauze or wadding. This is a soft, absorbent padding which has gauze either side so it doesn't tend to stick to the wound, unlike cotton wool and it can be cut to any shape or size. A pad can be used to cover the wound and attached with plastic tape. This wadding also makes excellent pads to clean and dry wounds; it has a multitude of uses
- Teabags for runny eyes, apparently this works a treat

- Buy your essentials from the supermarket like Sudocream, which is a great all round product to have in your vet box, it is essentially udder cream (zinc and castor oil) and is great as a barrier or protective cream and much cheaper to buy in your local supermarket (in the baby section) than an equine alternative at a local saddlery. Also sun protection cream, after sun, cotton wool and hair brushes for your grooming kit
- Do a First Aid course. These are often run by local veterinary practices. Straightforward wounds and injuries should be able to be managed by a competent horse owner, the essential skill is to know what you are dealing with. A good course should teach you how to differentiate the serious issue from the routine and basic skills such as how to dress a wound and apply a bandage. Get a more experienced friend to help you if you get stuck and share their skills
- Consider studying for the British Horse Society Stage examinations or the Horse Owner's Certificate. Knowledge is power and the more you understand about the horse's anatomy and how to care for it, the more proficient and competent you will become and this will in turn impact on your pocket

Bedding

The rule of thumb is to use the cheapest and most economical bedding for your pony, remember it all goes on the muck heap. If your Connemara pony has a dust issue then there is no point using straw even though it is one of the cheapest types of bedding, you will need to use a dust free or a dust extracted alternative, but there are a huge variety of different types available and great variations in price.

Economy comes in different forms. A more expensive bedding that you use less of will actually cost you less over the weeks than a cheaper bedding that you need to replace more frequently. If you are thinking about changing your pony's bedding then find someone who uses your potential new type and ask if you can go

Chapter 13: Costs

and see it in action, at least find out how many bales they use per week for comparison and then search online or via social media groups for the best and cheapest supplier in your area.

If you use wood shavings then you could contact your local joiners and collect wood shavings from them for free. If you store them first in a dustbin or in sacks and give it a good shake from time to time then the dust will accumulate at the bottom and can be discarded. Use this as the base for a shavings bed and then top up with the usual, more expensive equine shavings.

Consider using rubber matting, which although an initial outlay, is a one off cost that can help minimise the amount of bedding material that you may need to use going forward. The savings you make over the course of months in terms of bedding costs will easily outweigh the initial expense of the rubber mats, they will pay for themselves in no time.

Sometimes it is possible to source a bedding type that is used in a different environment and it can therefore be cheaper. The wooden pellets that are dampened for use can be bought from non-equine suppliers and there are significant savings to be made as they can be used as a fuel source as well and therefore attract a lower rate of VAT if bought under this label.

Deep littering is one option to reduce costs; this can save a fortune in bedding costs but does not suit every horse or environment. This may not be suitable if your Connemara pony has a respiratory issue.

Keeping the horse at grass for as long as possible is perhaps the simplest way to reduce bedding costs or even living out completely but again that is dependent on the amount of grazing available, the yard arrangements and whether that regime is suitable for your pony. And of course, if your pony does winter out with a field shelter, then you will need some sort of bedding or base in there over the colder months to prevent the ground from becoming churned up, but this is still a fraction of what it will cost you to bed down a stable. The longer your pony is out, the less bedding you will use and remember, this lifestyle is actually healthier for your pony anyway.

Some people are able to teach their horses to urinate or stale in a bucket on command. Goodness knows how! This will save a fortune in bedding.

Feeding

We all probably feed our horses too much, horses like dogs and cats and people too, are now carrying more weight than they did twenty or thirty years ago. It is a ticklish issue as horses need to eat continuously and we like to care for our horses, a fact which is not lost either on the feed companies or supplement manufacturers who are in the business of selling as much feed as possible. Remember the old adage "the eye of the master maketh the horse fat" and I guess what that means is, it is those that do the feeding which cause horses to be overweight, horses can only eat what we allow them to.

It is worth taking the time and trouble to understand some of the principles of correct feeding, because not only will you promote good health in your horse, you may save a bit of money too. Horses essentially need long fibre, and lots of it, so hay and grass in the first instance. Any additional hard feed should be based around work load and it is probably true to say that most owners over estimate how much work their horses are doing. Most horses can go a long way riding and competing off just good grass and hay and they are all the happier and healthier for it. And most of the causes of weight loss in the winter months are due to lack of fibre, but the temptation for many people is to increase hard feed first rather than hay. Horses don't get bored of just hay and grass, if you put them in a field they will eat the green stuff all day.

Nearly all the feed companies now provide advice lines and most also do yard visits where they can weigh your pony on a portable weighbridge, condition score the horse and, in conjunction with any underlying health conditions and workload, calculate the correct ration for your animal. These feeds are nutritionally balanced and so should remove the need for additional supplements and a handful of this and a handful of that; these extras may well be entirely superfluous, unnecessary, and possibly even harmful and all impact upon your pocket.

A balanced diet is all the average healthy horse needs unless the vet or farrier has identified the need for additional supplementation for a specific reason, such as poor hoof quality or some form of deficiency. A lot of people spend additional funds on costly additives that may already be present in the horses' feed or may simply not be necessary, purely because they don't really understand the science. If you have a large enough yard and can arrange a visit from a feed company to see several horses, then those owners will often get a free bag of feed as well.

Here are some specific tips.

- In the winter when we like to feed succulents, see if you can find someone who has unwanted windfall apples, they are probably only too happy for you to come and take them away
- Carrot nets are another popular option during the colder months, they vary in price from tack shop to feed merchants but if you can get in touch with the supplier and go and collect them, you will find them at a much cheaper rate or arrange a bulk delivery to your yard
- When feeding hay on the field, you can use old wooden tile crates, checking for protruding nails and sharp areas first. This helps contain the hay and means there is much less wastage

Watering

Use water butts to collect rain water for your Connemara pony, its free water and mineral rich, use it to water the horses, to soak hay and to wash tails.

Chapter 13: Costs

Your community

If you are on part or DIY livery, pooling your resources with your fellow owners is one of the best routes to saving money. If you can share the work between a few people on a rota system, then this not only creates time in your own life away from the yard but also saves you the fuel costs of travelling there and back.

Sharing travel if you have a lorry or trailer, buddying up with a friend on the yard to go to a show or maybe to the beach to ride, is a good way to save money. If you have to take your pony into the vet, is someone on the yard prepared to do it so that you can avoid the costs of professional transport hire? Paying fuel costs to a friend is not considered to be a commercial arrangement, but anything further is considered to be for hire and reward and therefore will become a commercial arrangement so do be careful if offering transport to a friend or making such an arrangement.

Using experts

Being able to share call out charges is one of the biggest benefits of being on a livery yard.

If you need to arrange the saddle fitter or the dentist to come out to your Connemara pony, then plan ahead and try and share the visit with as many other people as possible. This should make it cheaper for everyone, as you won't all incur an individual call out fee.

If you have good facilities and the yard owner is agreeable, you could consider offering the premises to your practitioner on say a monthly basis so that they can base themselves there for a day (or more frequently) and allow external people to visit them at your yard. You would need to make sure that this wasn't just a benefit for the yard owner though and that some financial reward or discount filters down to the livery owners. Of course the downside to this, is that it can tie up yard facilities when owners want to use them as well as the added complication of unknown horses coming into the yard.

Chapter 13: Costs

Sharing the cost of a veterinary call out for routine and planned work is a long established way of saving money. Some veterinary practises will offer a heavily discounted or free call out if you book the work on a zone day designated to your geographical area by the practise. If you have a big enough yard, you may be able to establish a set day or two per month when the vet is allocated to call and owners just book in their horses if they require attention, this will usually result in a very discounted or zero charge call out. Do shop around as veterinary charges can vary enormously from practice to practice.

If you don't have your Connemara pony based on a big yard, you are perhaps on your own renting land or you have your horses at home, then using Social Media, it is possible to coordinate visits from equine professionals to cover several people in the area or even to offer your own premises as a base for the day for local owners to bring their horses in. There are so many horsey groups on Facebook that sourcing and making contact with people who live near you, has never been easier.

Bulk deliveries can also be arranged via this route – hard feed, bedding, hay - negotiate a discount for a large order for your yard or people in your area.

Discuss with your farrier if your pony really does need to wear shoes or can he do without them for part if not all of the year. Are there times when your pony is doing less work and even the hind shoes can be removed? All the savings soon add up, although your Connemara pony will still need to be trimmed at regular intervals of anywhere from six to eight weeks, even if he is not wearing shoes.

Shop around for different veterinary practices. Routine charges can vary considerably from practice to practice and it is worth finding out what other practices in your area charge. Social media can be a good source of information in this regard as in addition to charges, you should also be able to get a feel for quality of service and people's experiences, both good and bad.

Chapter 13: Costs

Remember that a healthy horse is cheaper to keep than a sick horse so you should never hesitate to call the vet out if you think it is necessary. Owners who treat horses themselves because they have taken a guess at what they think the problem is, often end up costing themselves more money in the long run, not to mention the welfare implications for the horse.

Chapter 14: Travelling horses

Chapter 14: Travelling horses

Many owners have their own transport for their horses, particularly helpful if you compete regularly but great to be able to travel horses to the beach or the forest to hack or when they need to go into the vet.

There are two ways to transport horses which are:-

- A trailer attached to a towing vehicle
- A horsebox or lorry

Horse Trailers

A horse trailer is essentially a wheeled box which is attached to a suitable vehicle and towed. It has no independent mechanical mechanism. There are several different manufacturing companies in the UK which make trailers, Ifor Williams, Richardson and Equitrek are probably the main three and they all offer something slightly different to the horse owner. If you are unfamiliar with travelling horses then speak to friends or even people at shows and ask if you can look at their trailer, find out what they like and don't like about it. Here are some of the principle points to consider when buying a trailer:-

- Do you want a left or right unload. These days most trailers unload at the front although there are some bigger models that look like mini horse boxes and they have a ramp at the side. Ifor Williams unload to the right and Richardson to the left. The theory is that the left unload is technically safer as you can unload onto the side of the road in an emergency away from the traffic whereas with an Ifor Williams, you would be unloading into the traffic in an emergency. A great theory, that is unless you are in a country lane and by a verge or hedge

Chapter 14: Travelling horses

- How many horses do you need to carry and what size are they? You will need a long enough trailer with sufficient headroom for your horse
- Most trailers are stalled to carry two horses either facing forwards or backwards and are split with a central partition. Can you remove the partition and does the trailer have full length bars? Some horses will not travel with the partition in and become very stressed. They will however travel with the partition out and then tend to stand diagonally on the vehicle, this is when you need the full length breast bars and rear bars. Being able to remove the partitions and travel one horse or even two, e.g. mare and foal in a different position, is always very helpful
- Do you prefer a wooden or an aluminum floor? Some people are very hesitant about wooden floors due to the fear of them rotting over time from the continuous effect of the horse's urine and therefore will opt for a metal floor. However, all floors should be checked regularly by a competent garage that can put the trailer up on a ramp and look at it from the underneath. The trailers with wooden floors seem to give the horse a smoother ride with less jolting
- What towing vehicle do you have? The towing vehicle must itself be of an adequate weight and have sufficient braking capacity to support the combined weight of your trailer and its occupants. Different towing vehicles could themselves occupy the content of an entire new publication and it is not the remit of this book to look at these
- Does your driving licence allow you to tow? In the UK, all people who passed their driving test after the 1st January 1997 need to take an additional test to be allowed to tow a trailer legally. Towing can be quite challenging, going forward is alright but maneuvering and parking takes some expertise, so even if you do not require any formal trailer training by law, you might wish to consider some

Chapter 14: Travelling horses

training before you start towing, as it can prove to be quite a daunting experience

Horseboxes

A horsebox is a motorized lorry so it is one complete unit. Horseboxes can vary from the quite basic to top of the range models costing over £100,000 ($156,840.00). These have living accommodation including sleeping facilities, kitchen and shower. Again you need to look carefully at your budget and how many horses you need to carry and for what distance. Some horseboxes that do a lot of small trips may not have a requirement for any accommodation or kitchen so more space can be given over to carrying horses. It is always really useful though to have a small kitchen area.

The same date of the 1st January 1997 again is significant. If you passed your driving test in the UK prior to that date then you can legally drive up to 7.5 tonnes on your car licence. After that date and the legal limit is 3.5 tonnes.

One of the main issues in the UK is with horseboxes that hover around the magic weight of 7.5 tonnes. If you want to carry two or three big horses and people plus tack and water, you would be correct in thinking that you would need a pretty lightweight lorry to come in at under 7.5 tonnes and you are right. Modern or newer lorries which are built in materials that are strong but lightweight can achieve this but older lorries are often as much as 5 tonnes unladen. It is therefore absolutely imperative that you get a kerb or parking weight for the lorry when it is unladen before you consider purchase otherwise you may well find yourself overweight when your horses are in transit. If you are stopped by "VOSA" the Vehicle Operator and Services Agency which is the regulatory body in the UK at the roadside, they can require you to shed items until you come in underweight, you certainly will not be allowed to continue your journey if you are overweight. Because of the requirement to have further training if you are driving a vehicle which is over 7.5 tonnes when laden, there is some small incentive of vendors of used vehicles which carry 2 or

3 horses to present their lorry as being under the magic level of 7.5 tonnes so shop with caution.

If you want to drive vehicles that are over 7.5 tonnes then you are entering the realm of Heavy Goods Vehicles and will need to obtain an additional licence called an HGV licence. This requires training which takes around 4 days and will cost in the region of £1,000($1,568.29).

Buying a horsebox or trailer

The key really is to take advice rather as with buying a horse. If you don't know anything about it then find experienced help. There is a thriving used market in horseboxes and trailers but it really is buyer beware. Car accidents are bad enough but an accident that involves a vehicle containing horses is horrendous so you have a huge responsibility to make sure that the vehicle you are buying is roadworthy or, if you are buying something with issues, that you know what they are and can rectify them.

Maintenance

Trailers are usually simpler to look after than horseboxes as they have no engine. Here are some things that you need to check on a regular basis:-

- Tyres. They need to be in good condition and check regularly for wear or damage including splitting. Tyre pressures need to be the correct amount for your trailer and the position of the wheel on the trailer. Over inflated tyres will burst and under inflated tyres will at the very least increase your fuel consumption as there is more drag on the towing vehicle, but they can also split causing a blow out so potentially, this can be very dangerous as well. Always carry a spare which is usually fitted to the side of the trailer and check that regularly as well for roadworthiness
- Lights. These are powered by a cable connection to the towing vehicle. Connect them and check that they are in

working order on a regular basis even if you are not using the trailer
- The floor. Lift the matting on a regular basis if possible and look at the condition of the floor. The trailer floor should be viewed from beneath at least once a year by a garage or mechanic
- The fittings and closing pins. Make sure that all the fittings are in good working order and move efficiently and easily, repair or replace any that do not
- Brakes. The trailer will have its own braking system and this should be checked annually when the floor is looked at and any worn pads and cabling replaced
- If you do not use the trailer regularly to carry horses, make sure you hitch it up and take it for a run occasionally, particularly during the winter months. This keeps the running gear and brake mechanism working smoothly

Horseboxes, because they are a motorized vehicle, are treated like any other haulage vehicle on the road and have their own annual test to check that they are roadworthy, much like the MOT for a car in the UK. This test is called plating. As with a trailer, this annual test does not absolve you from the need to regularly check and maintain your horsebox and keep it in good repair. The floor, fittings, brakes, lights and steering should all be monitored for signs of wear and tear and any defects remedied as soon as they appear.

Travelling horses

Preparing the horse to travel
It is personal preference as to what a horse wears when travelling, some people prefer to use little protection as if an item becomes loose or partly detached from the horse, this can cause a much more serious incident than a bang or a knock incurred whilst in transit. Here are some items that you might consider using and these apply equally whether you are travelling your horse on a horsebox or a trailer:-

Chapter 14: Travelling horses

- A leather head collar. This is essential so that it will break in the event of an accident. Remember that the horse should always be tied to a small loop of baler twine both when inside the vehicle and when tied up to the outside of it at a show or event
- Poll guard. This is to protect the top of the horse's head and is particularly useful with difficult loaders who may be inclined to rear. It is a padded section, usually of sheepskin, which fits over the top of the horse's head collar
- Rug or summer sheet depending on the temperature. Horses do get very hot when travelling, they have to work to balance and so do not be tempted to over rug
- Protection on the legs either with travelling bandages or travel boots
- Tail bandage and or tail guard. Some horses lean back and balance on the back bar when they are travelling and can rub their tails. A tail bandage should not be left on for more than four hours at a time so would not be a suitable choice for a long journey

Loading

Some horses do have issues with travelling and either do not load well or do not travel well or both. However, it is also fair to say that a lot of issues are manmade when it comes to difficult loaders. If you are not experienced or you think you may have difficulties with a particular horse then get someone competent to help you.

Some horses load better in a bridle, it gives you more control if they are being difficult and can be removed once they are on board. Using a lunge line can also help rather than a lead rope, as again it gives you more options when handling a difficult horse. For safety, you should always wear a hat and gloves when loading and sensible footwear that will not slip.

When travelling a sole horse on a trailer, they would load onto the right hand side so they are effectively behind the driver; this gives

Chapter 14: Travelling horses

the horse a better ride as it will be less affected by the camber on the road. For this reason, some people in the UK prefer left unload trailers as it is easier for a sole big horse to unload to the left than the right. On a lorry, a single horse goes on at the back, so it is standing over the back axle, which offers a better distribution of weight.

If you have a difficult loader then seek experienced or professional help. If you are unsure or lack confidence then you will only make the situation worse and either you or the horse may end up being injured.

Driving horses
The golden rule is that you cannot do anything suddenly so no sharp turns or braking as the horse will stumble and may fall over. Imagine driving an unboxed wedding cake of several tiers on the back seat of your car and you will have some idea of the experience! It takes practice to tow horses, probably more difficult in many ways than driving a horse box, as you have two vehicles to consider so practice for a time with an empty vehicle until you feel confident. Spend some time out and about with an empty vehicle and a friend who is an experienced driver who can offer you some tips and advice. If you are upgrading from a trailer to a horsebox, again spend some time driving it around empty so you get used to the size and feel of the vehicle. It is probably always advisable to take someone with you when you are taking horses out as if you have a problem or an accident, another pair of hands can be essential.

Breakdown cover

In the event that you have a problem with your towing vehicle, trailer or horsebox, you need to consider what you will do with the horses. Recovering vehicles is straightforward enough but recovery and breakdown companies will not routinely offer assistance with the horses unless you have specific cover in place for this.

Chapter 14: Travelling horses

Some people rely on friends to help out in a crisis, particularly if they only travel locally, but you can be vulnerable if you travel horses further afield and you do also run the risk of getting stuck if your friends are not available to help out. Keep a list of local equine transport companies in the cab with their phone numbers. Or you could consider joining a specific breakdown company, which will recover your vehicle in the event of an accident or breakdown and also arrange for your horses to be collected and transported with overnight livery as well if you are far from home. This offers great peace of mind. In the UK there is an organization called the OHTO which is the Organisation of Horsebox and Trailer Owners which offer this type of service as well as general information about the different rules and regulations which surround towing or driving horseboxes.

Conclusion

Owning a horse or pony is a truly unique experience. As I slide around in the mud and ice in the winter months, I wonder why on earth I do it sometimes. I have yet to be able to put into words the unique hold that these animals have over humans and the precious bond that we form with them.

In 2014, the subject of the Annual Conference for World Horse Welfare "WHW" the international rescue and rehabilitation charity held in London was, "the value of the horse". This debate covered many areas of discussion around financial value and consequent welfare issues but there were two particularly moving and thought provoking speeches, one given by a writer and philosopher Roger Scruton who had discovered horses later in life, his comments were so well observed and humourous. And the closing speech from a man called Jason Hare who as a Royal Marine, had suffered life changing injuries following two bomb blasts whilst he was on active service in Iraq with the British Army. Without a trace of self- pity, Jason described the effect that horses had had on him as part of his rehabilitation at a special centre in Scotland, a very moving and humbling speech.

Whatever your journey with your new horse or pony, you will be guaranteed fun, excitement, cost, thrills and spills and more along the way. There is a tremendous camaraderie in the horse world linked as we all are by this very special creature and there will always be someone ready to help you out or share your highs and lows so all that remains for me to say is, welcome aboard!

"There is something about the outside of a horse that is good for the inside of a man". Winston Churchill

Glossary

CPBS	Connemara Pony Breeders Society
BHS	British Horse Society
FEC	Faecal egg count
RCVS	Royal College of Veterinary Surgeons
PIO	Passport Issuing Organisation
BEVA	British Equine Veterinary Association
DEFRA	Department for the Environment, Food and Rural Affairs
WHW	World Horse Welfare
VOSA	Vehicle Operator and Standards Agency
OHTO	Organisation of Horsebox and Trailer Owners

Published by IMB Publishing 2015

Copyright and Trademarks: This publication is Copyrighted 2015 by IMB Publishing. All products, publications, software and services mentioned and recommended in this publication are protected by trademarks. In such instance, all trademarks & copyright belong to the respective owners. All rights reserved. No part of this book may be reproduced or transferred in any form or by any means, graphic, electronic, or mechanical, including photocopying, recording, taping, or by any information storage retrieval system, without the written permission of the authors. Pictures used in this book are either royalty free pictures bought from stock-photo websites or have the source mentioned underneath the picture.

Disclaimer and Legal Notice: This product is not legal or medical advice and should not be interpreted in that manner. You need to do your own due-diligence to determine if the content of this product is right for you. The author and the affiliates of this product are not liable for any damages or losses associated with the content in this product. While every attempt has been made to verify the information shared in this publication, neither the author nor the affiliates assume any responsibility for errors, omissions or contrary interpretation of the subject matter herein. Any perceived slights to any specific person(s) or organization(s) are purely unintentional. We have no control over the nature, content and availability of the web sites listed in this book. The inclusion of any web site links does not necessarily imply a recommendation or endorse the views expressed within them. IMB Publishing takes no responsibility for, and will not be liable for, the websites being temporarily unavailable or being removed from the Internet. The accuracy and completeness of information provided herein and opinions stated herein are not guaranteed or warranted to produce any particular results, and the advice and strategies, contained herein may not be suitable for every individual. The author shall not be liable for any loss incurred as a consequence of the use and application, directly or indirectly, of any information presented in this work. This publication is designed to provide information in regards to the subject matter covered. The information included in this book has been compiled to give an overview of the subject s and detail some of the symptoms, treatments etc. that are available to people with this condition. It is not intended to give medical advice. For a firm diagnosis of your condition, and for a treatment plan suitable for you, you should consult your doctor or consultant. The writer of this book and the publisher are not responsible for any damages or negative consequences following any of the treatments or methods highlighted in this book. Website links are for informational purposes and should not be seen as a personal endorsement; the same applies to the products detailed in this book. The reader should also be aware that although the web links included were correct at the time of writing, they may become out of date in the future.

Printed in Great Britain
by Amazon